The best prescriptic

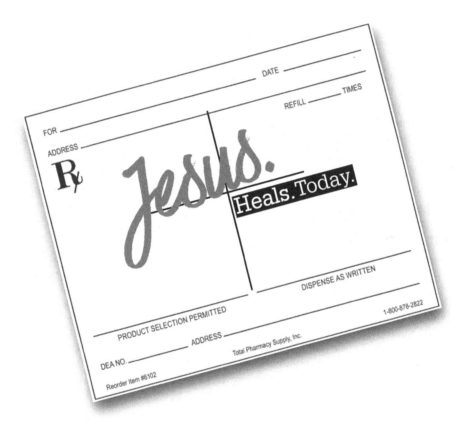

Dianne Leman and Putty Putman

Published by: fox and hare publications

ISBN 13: 978-1985121850

Scriptures marked ESV are taken from the THE HOLY BIBLE, ENGLISH
STANDARD VERSION (ESV): Scriptures taken from THE HOLY BIBLE,
ENGLISH STANDARD VERSION ® Copyright© 2001 by Crossway, a
publishing ministry of Good News Publishers. Used by permission.

Scriptures marked NASB are taken from the NEW AMERICAN STANDARD
BIBLE (NASB): Scripture taken from the NEW AMERICAN STANDARD
BIBLE®, Copyright© 1960, 1962, 1963, 1968, 1971, 1972, 1973, 1975, 1977, 1995 by
The Lockman Foundation. Used by permission.

Scriptures marked NKJV are taken from the NEW KING JAMES VERSION
(NKJV): Scripture taken from the NEW KING JAMES VERSION®. Copyright©
1982 by Thomas Nelson, Inc. Used by permission. All rights reserved.

Scriptures marked NLT are taken from the HOLY BIBLE, NEW LIVING
TRANSLATION (NLT): Scriptures taken from the HOLY BIBLE, NEW LIVING
TRANSLATION, Copyright© 1996, 2004, 2007 by Tyndale House Foundation.
Used by permission of Tyndale House Publishers, Inc., Carol Stream, Illinois
60188. All rights reserved. Used by permission.

Cover Design: Katie Goulet
Interior Design: Jody Boles
Editing: Shelly Manning

http://dianneleman.com

http://puttyputman.com

fox and hare publications

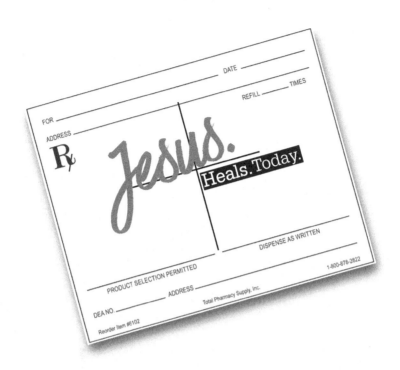

On the prescription pad:
FOR
ADDRESS
DATE
REFILL _____ TIMES
Jesus. Heals.Today.
DISPENSE AS WRITTEN
PRODUCT SELECTION PERMITTED
ADDRESS
DEA NO.
Total Pharmacy Supply, Inc.
1-800-878-2822
Reorder Item #6102

Dedication

To
Jesus, our Great Physician
and
All who need His healing touch today

God anointed Jesus of Nazareth with the Holy Spirit and with power.
He went about doing good and healing all who were oppressed
by the devil, for God was with Him. Acts 10:38

Table of Contents

Introduction

The Best Prescription

Jesus.Heals.Today.

Jesus, God incarnate, heals—makes one well—today, right here, right now. Really? I mean, Jesus is not exactly here on earth taking medical appointments. How does Jesus heal today? Good question. That is what this book is all about.

When we say, "Jesus heals today," we get a variety of responses from people. Maybe you can identify with one or more of these:

"Oh, yes, I am so thankful for all the advanced medicines and expert physicians that are available today in the 21st Century. Jesus heals through all of these."

"Yes, I know Jesus heals today—but sometimes He wants us to stay sick and suffer to teach us a lesson. We should not be presumptuous."

"Wait, I thought that was just in the 'olden days,' you know, in the Bible, that Jesus healed people. Are you saying it still happens today?"

"OK, I believe Jesus could heal today, but why don't I ever see it? There are huge hospital complexes all over the place that surely would not be needed if Jesus were really healing today. Right?"

"I once believed that Jesus heals today but too many people that have received prayer for healing have not gotten better and some have actually died."

"Yes! I know Jesus heals today. I want to learn more about this and experience Jesus' healing for myself and others."

This final response is the one we embrace and we will take six chapters to explore in *Jesus.Heals.Today.* Because you chose this book, we assume you at least have an interest in, or are open to the fact that Jesus, God Himself, is still healing the sick today, just like He did while He walked on the earth over 2000 years ago. Our hope is each one of you will come away with fresh faith in Jesus' deep desire for you, your family and your friends to be healthy and whole. We, like Jesus, are eager for you to experience Jesus' healing power for yourself and turn and share with others who are hurting. Healing is a hot topic. It is very much needed and yet remarkably elusive for so many. Jesus knows our needs and is ready to provide His help. Jesus is the best prescription for a hurting world.

Healing is Much Needed

In the 21st Century there are many medical treatment options available and yet a large number of people are still sick. Actually, we are very sick, according to a large-scale inventory of global illness levels. More than 95% of the world's population is ill, the new analysis based on the 2013 Global Burden of Disease Study found. What's more, one-third of those had more than five chronic or acute illnesses. The study, published in The Lancet, examined and evaluated chronic and acute disease and injury across 188 countries from 1990 to 2013.*

We are sick people. Healing is desperately needed. We need healing. Our family, friends and those around us need healing. We are thankful for all the medical advances in curing diseases and we are grateful to the dedicated men and women who practice medicine. We do not take a dualistic approach—separating the spiritual, supernatural and the natural or physical. But we do have an amazing Father who knows our need, knows how to heal every disease, wants His children well and wants us to be convinced that Jesus heals us today.

---

* https://www.sciencedaily.com/releases/2015/06/150608081753.htm

Healing is desperately needed. We need healing. Our family, friends and those around us need healing. We are thankful for all the medical advances in curing diseases and we are grateful to the dedicated men and women who practice medicine. We do not take a dualistic approach—separating the spiritual, supernatural and the natural or physical. But we do have an amazing Father who knows our need, knows how to heal every disease, wants His children well and wants us to be convinced that Jesus heals us today.

Healing is Complex

Healing is a very complex issue. I wish healing was as simple as "do this or do that and you will be healed!" Or as simple as saying, "I believe Jesus heals," (although that is a good start). But the human body itself is quite complex with all its various systems, organs, and functions. Then, when we consider each person's emotional, mental, environmental, relational, spiritual and genetic makeup, we confront the complexity and challenge of getting a person healed and staying healthy. In addition, there are multitudes of serious illnesses and diseases for which there is no available cure from modern medicine despite mounds of research, medications and therapies. We live in a world that is no longer simple due to advancing science and technology that both help and hinder our lives. The global and cosmic nature of our universe can be overwhelming. We are a complicated creation living in a complicated world. Healing is truly complex. But we have a compassionate Father who created the universe, created the human body and best knows how to heal us and keep us healthy. He wants us to know and experience this simple truth in our complex world: Jesus heals today.

Healing is Expensive

Then, there is the money. Billions of dollars are spent in research, treatments, medicines and of course, health insurance. Currently, Americans pay $3.4 trillion a year for medical care (and, unfortunately, don't get impressive results). According to the most recent data available from the Centers for Medicare and Medicaid Services (CMS), "The average American spent $9,596 on healthcare" in 2012, which was "up significantly from $7,700 in 2007." It was also more than twice the per capita average of other developed nations, but still, in 2015, experts predicted continued sharp increases. Indeed, average annual costs per person hit $10,345 in 2016. In 1960, the average cost per person was only $146–and, adjusting for inflation, that means costs are nine times higher now than they were then.*

Healing is expensive and costs continue to rise. This is rocking our nation, rocking our own lives. While desperate financial pressure cannot be our only motivation for seeking help, we do have a loving Father who makes it so clear that He wants us well and generously gives His children healing and health. His provision is: Jesus heals today–without price, without cost.

We need healing. We need help for the complex, expensive dilemma of sickness and disease. We need more than earthly solutions, as good as they may be. We need heavenly help. We need to know and experience for ourselves that Jesus heals today.

I Know Jesus Heals Today

This truth, that Jesus heals today, radically changed my life over forty years ago and I have lived in the reality of His healing power for myself and others ever since. As a pastor, mother and grandmother, I have personally witnessed Jesus' powerful healing over and over. But this forty-year journey has not been without many questions, some disappointments and discouragement and even some difficult heartaches. However, I am more convinced than ever that Jesus heals today and is eager for us to trust His love and faithfulness. And, I am more convinced than ever that given the current health crisis in our world, we now need a bold and believable encounter with the Jesus who heals today. I, along

---

*https://www.cnbc.com/2017/06/23/heres-how-much-the-average-american-spends-on-health-care.html

with my co-author Putty Putman, will look at what the Bible teaches, share the lessons we have learned, and expect the Holy Spirit to reveal everything we need to experience Jesus and His healing love and power. We want all to know, experience and pass on–Jesus heals today.

Join Us on a Journey of Healing

Here is what you can expect in the following chapters of *Jesus.Heals. Today*:

Introduction – The Best Prescription (*Dianne*)

- You are reading it!

Chapter 1 – Jesus is the Best Doctor (*Dianne*)

- Jesus is not the only doctor, but He is the best.
- Start experiencing His amazing healthcare, today.

Chapter 2 – Jesus Conquered Sickness (*Putty*)

- Why aren't my prayers for healing answered? There is a cosmic war happening.
- Learn how to engage and experience more of Jesus' healing power for yourself and others
- Jesus' victory over sickness is in effect today.

Chapter 3 – Jesus Honors Faith (*Dianne*)

- Jesus mentions faith in respect to healing over twenty times. How do I have faith? What is faith?
- Learn to be a person who lives by faith and experience Jesus' healing for yourself, your family and friends.
- Jesus still honors faith today.

Chapter 4 – Jesus Heals Miraculously (*Putty*)

- Miracles can be mysterious but Jesus clearly does miracles and shows us some of His secrets.
- See Him in action and get ready to receive your miracle.
- Jesus is still doing miracles today.

Chapter 5 – Jesus Wants Us Whole (*Dianne*)

- We are an integrated being and therefore, all parts of our being are involved in our health. It is not just a matter of getting our body well, but also our mind and spirit as well.
- Learn that Jesus wants us whole and how to receive His healing.
- Jesus wants us whole today.

Chapter 6 – Jesus Send Us to Heal (*Putty*)

- Healing is never just for us alone, but always to pass on to others, showing them Jesus' love and power.
- Learn how to simply, naturally, yet supernaturally, pray for others to be made whole through the power of the Holy Spirit.
- Jesus sends us to heal the sick in His name today.

Conclusion – A Lifelong Journey (*Putty*)

- Final thoughts
- Resources

Appendix

- Sample Prayers

There are many aspects of Jesus' healing that we do not cover in these six short chapters. We highly recommend that you use the accompanying Jesus. Heals. Today. message series and DVD with teaching and testimonies that supplement these chapters. This is excellent for a whole church or just a small group to do together. These resources are available at **http://store.schoolofkingdomministry.org.** If you would like to do a more thorough study, please see our list of other books and teachings on our resource page. My personal favorite resource on healing is the Bible, especially the four Gospels, Matthew, Mark, Luke and John which show, without question, that Jesus wants us well. The Gospel of Mark opens right away with the awesome picture of Jesus' desire to heal:

A man with leprosy came and knelt in front of Jesus, begging to be healed. "If you are willing, you can heal me and make me clean," he said.

Moved with compassion, Jesus reached out and touched him. "I am willing," he said. "Be healed!" Instantly the leprosy disappeared, and the man was healed. Mark 1:40-42 NLTs

This is the heart of Jesus, the same Jesus who still heals today. Let's find out how to experience this for ourselves and others. Let's encounter the healing compassion and power of Jesus. Join us on an exciting journey of healing.

Going with you....

Dianne Leman and Putty Putman

January 2018

Chapter **1**

Jesus is
the Best Doctor

A Surprising Discovery

"I'm sorry Mr. and Mrs. Leman," the prestigious Chicago physician said with somber, but gentle, authority. "Our tests show that it is very unlikely you could ever conceive your own child. I treat infertility with the best, most advanced medical options available today and our advice to you, in light of what we have discovered, is please consider adopting a child."

While those words were the devastating conclusion of a long, expensive, painful and heartbreaking journey, they were also the words that put my husband and me on a radical life changing path—a path of discovering that Jesus heals today and that Jesus is the best doctor. Yes, Jesus is the best doctor. He is not the only doctor, but He is the best doctor. In saying this, I am not saying I am against medical treatment or that I am ungrateful for all the wonderful doctors, nurses and medical personnel who work hard to bring healing to the sick and hurting.

No, I am saying I discovered something I never knew for 27 years of my life, despite being raised in a Christian home and church. I discovered Jesus heals today and He is the smartest, most powerful, most compassionate physician ever. The outcome of that journey was a miraculous (even called such by the doctor) healing from infertility, the birth of five healthy children and a growing gang of grandchildren. In addition, we embraced the unexpected career change from business and education to pastoring. For over forty years we have led a church that believes, teaches and experiences the healing power of Jesus. We are convinced that Jesus heals today, both from God's Word and from our experience. We believe Jesus is the best doctor.

More to Learn

It has not been an entirely smooth journey. We have prayed for people who did not get better and some who even died too early. We have witnessed many people being healed from cancer, infertility, deafness, back pain, migraines and hundreds of other conditions. Yet, we have been stymied by unanswered prayers and have been tempted to quit–quit believing that Jesus heals today and quit praying for others to be healed. Every person is unique and there are no formulas for healing. The challenging factors in today's world add another layer of complexity. But, through it all, the Holy Spirit has been faithful to bring encouragement to us to stay the course and continue to trust Jesus and His desire to make us whole. Do we have all the answers? No, but we know Jesus does. Do we still have much to learn? Yes, but there is one question whose answer we know for sure. When we ask, "Is it God's will to heal?" our answer is "Absolutely, yes." But, as Putty shares in Chapter 2, the will of God is not always done on earth or in our bodies because there is a cosmic war. Despite the battle, we are convinced the Father wants His children well. Healing is the will of our good God, our good Father.

The Father's Will is Healing for All

How can we know for sure that it is God's will to heal? That was my question as I battled through years of infertility. Then my eyes were opened by the Holy Spirit to see that Jesus exactly reflects the Father and His will. Throughout His three years of ministry on earth, Jesus spent a significant amount of time healing people. Jesus clearly revealed that the Father's heart and will is healing for all. Over and over we read texts like,

> And he went throughout all Galilee, teaching in their synagogues and proclaiming the gospel of the kingdom and healing every disease and every affliction among the people. So his fame spread throughout all Syria, and they brought him all the sick, those afflicted with various diseases and pains, those oppressed by demons, those having seizures, and paralytics, and he healed them. Matthew 4:23-24 ESV

Jesus healed every disease and every affliction. What an amazing doctor! He never turned anyone away and no infirmity was too difficult for Him. And, like any good doctor, He certainly never told anyone to keep suffering in their sickness to learn some unknown lesson, nor did He intentionally make anyone sick so God would be glorified.

This was standard operating procedure for Jesus as He announced and then demonstrated that the Kingdom of God, the dynamic rule of God, had arrived on earth in His Person and ministry. Jesus healed every disease and every affliction. What an amazing doctor! He never turned anyone away and no infirmity was too difficult for Him. And, like any good doctor, He certainly never told anyone to keep suffering in their sickness to learn some unknown lesson, nor did He intentionally make anyone sick so God would be glorified. Yet these are theologies perpetrated today about God's use of sickness and suffering to "grow us up." This theology destroys faith in the Father's compassionate desire to heal, not harm. Such twisted theology paints a cruel caricature of God as a punishing, abusive Father who, unlike any decent earthly father, uses sickness to train His children. Ironically, the same people who embrace these unbiblical teachings are also ones who continue to pursue medical help and healing. My response to them is, if God is really teaching lessons through sickness, suffering and pain, it would not be wise to thwart God's teaching by taking medicine or getting treatment.

Of course, such logic is lost as people speak out of two sides of their mouths. No, our Father is a good Father, a compassionate Father, a loving Father. He gives good gifts to His children—gifts of healing, wholeness and health. He gave us Jesus, the best doctor, who showed us the Father's heart and will. And this has been the heart of the Father forever.

The Lord, Our Healer

Although Jesus' healing power was unusually strong and startling, the phenomenon of miraculous, supernatural healing was not new to the Jewish people in first century Israel. The tradition of God as Healer was revealed thousands of years before when the Israelite people were making their exodus from the oppression in Egypt. God revealed Himself as "the Lord, your Healer."

> And He said, "If you will give earnest heed to the voice of the LORD your God, and do what is right in His sight, and give ear to His commandments, and keep all His statutes, I will put none of the diseases on you which I have put on the Egyptians; for I, the LORD, am your Healer." Exodus 15:26 NASB

Throughout the Old Testament we read of God's healing power demonstrated through the prophets, priests and the people's covenant obedience. People were healed of infertility, leprosy, boils, poisoning and some were even raised from the dead. God's heart has always been for His children to be free from sickness and live long, healthy lives. In the beginning, He made us, human beings, in His very own image and gave us a deep desire to be whole. Such a desire within us simply reflects the nature and character of our Creator who has revealed Himself as the Lord, our Healer.

In the spring of 2016, I was at the University of Iowa Medical Center in Iowa City where my ninety-year-old mother was being treated for cancer of the mouth. Waiting for her to recover from the anesthesia, I wandered around this massive array of multi storied buildings that were filled with millions of dollars of equipment, machines and medicines. While I was overwhelmed by the enormity and complexity of the hospital, I was even more cut to the core by the desperation I saw on the faces of parents pushing pale children in wheelchairs or by the obvious fear that gripped families as they huddled in the waiting rooms. Haggard looking men pushed their IVs down the long halls alongside young women in hospital gowns, willing their injured legs to walk. So much desperation for healing. So much fragile hope. So much desire to see loved ones made well. Yes! That desire and hope is from God Himself who made each one of us in His own image and designed us to live whole and healthy lives. He is God, the Great Physician who designed our bodies to be healthy. And yes, He has gifted men and women through the centuries to discover wonderful cures and execute amazing medical miracles that have saved thousands of lives. Thank God for the many dedicated doctors. Jesus is not the only doctor, but there is no question, He is the best doctor today and He knows best how to heal the bodies He designed.

> So much desire to see loved ones made well. Yes! That desire and hope is from God Himself who made each one of us in His own image and designed us to live whole and healthy lives. He is God, the Great Physician who designed our bodies to be healthy.

Go to the Maker

When our ten-year-old Ford Pinto station wagon broke down, we were tempted to run it over to the local gas station for a quick fix. That would have been a big mistake that left us with a big bill and a still broken car. We needed to take that unique vehicle to a Ford dealer who had mechanics trained to fix Ford vehicles with Ford parts. While that is a corny example, it nevertheless illustrates my point that we really should trust the one who made us to direct the healing of our bodies when something goes wrong. Not only is Jesus the best doctor, but He is the One who designed the very bodies we are asking Him to heal. He is our Maker! A simple study of human anatomy and the way our body functions leaves us in awe of how intricate, how meticulous and how miraculous a human being really is. And to make sure we stay healthy, God even made sure we have our very own built in healing system—our immune system. This marvel protects us from who knows how many sicknesses and diseases in any given day and marshals healing when an invasion of trouble occurs. Aren't you glad the best doctor is the one who actually designed and created our bodies, even created them to handle sickness and disease? And, when our immune system cannot handle a specific problem, Jesus is ready to prescribe for us how to get well. When sickness strikes, I say, "Go to God first." Yes, let's go to our Maker who truly understands our entire being. As simple as that sounds, it is not that easy! That's because there are at least five different factors at play when we are seeking healing and looking to Jesus as the best doctor. I like to call them the "D" factors because they all start with the letter D: Devil, Disease, Divine Help, Doctors, Decisions. Our understanding of these five factors is very important and their interaction makes a big difference is how we experience healing.

God Heals, Not Harms

"God decided to close your womb," offered my well-meaning Christian friend in response to my question of God's plan for my life. "You are such a great special education teacher and God knows those children really need you. They will be 'your children' instead of your own." I wanted to scream in her face and tell her I did not like God's plan. I wanted children of my own and a classroom full of wonderful children was no substitute for my own flesh and blood. I was not sure I could continue to worship a God who was so capricious in opening and closing wombs and who played favorites. How thankful I am that God not only opened my womb, but He first opened my eyes to see that He is the Giver of Life, not the taker. He is the one who blesses the womb, not makes it barren. God heals, not harms. No, there is another player on the field. There is a real enemy. His name is the devil. And I spent twenty-seven years of my life not knowing he was real, he is powerful and he, not God, is the author of sickness, sin and sorrow. Yes, the devil is a factor to be noted when we seek healing.

> God heals, not harms. No, there is another player on the field. There is a real enemy. His name is the devil. And I spent twenty-seven years of my life not knowing he was real, he is powerful and he, not God, is the author of sickness, sin and sorrow.

Five Factors

Disease and sickness were not always here on earth. There was no sickness in the original creation, before humans were tempted by the devil and sinned. And there will be no sickness when the Kingdom comes in all its fullness at the completion of this age and the devil is defeated and destroyed forever. But now, as we live in the tension of God's Kingdom here, but not yet here in fullness, we must contend with the devil, the author of sickness and disease and enforce the victory Jesus won at the cross. Putty will address this more fully in Chapter 2 but for now, I note this to establish these two important factors:

- Disease-This was never God's will and He is not causing your disease or sending it on you.

- Devil-There is a real devil and he is behind all disease which is a result of the fall of all creation into sin. He is responsible directly or indirectly for all disease.

Once you are certain that God is not sending you the disease and you know the devil is a real being, you are better equipped to receive your healing. Here are where the next three factors come in:

- Divine help-It has always been and is still available for healing. God is the original doctor and as I have been saying, He is the best doctor.

- Doctors-Human doctors have long been gifted to bring healing through many different means throughout history. We can receive wonderful help from them, but our ultimate trust should be in Jesus, the best doctor.

- Decisions-Our decisions about all of the above, plus lifestyle choices, are important. What we decide to believe and do with the other four factors will make a difference in our healing. God is quite good at honoring our choices and will let us decide many things with or without His help.

There are other healing factors to consider, especially the cosmic war Putty discusses in Chapter 2 which definitely relates to the devil factor in many ways. However, as we establish that Jesus is the best doctor, these five Ds are foundational.

There is a passage in the Bible, recorded by a physician, Dr. Luke, that reflects the interplay of these factors. Luke was a medical doctor who wrote the Gospel of Luke and travelled with the early apostles. Throughout his Gospel he records many of Jesus' healings. As a doctor, Luke never maligns medical help except he notes one time that a sick woman had spent all her money on physicians without getting better (see Luke 7:43). He also authored the Book of Acts and summarized Jesus' healing ministry this way:

> And you know that God anointed Jesus of Nazareth with the Holy Spirit and with power. Then Jesus went around doing good and healing all who were oppressed by the devil, for God was with him. Acts 10:38 NLT

The *doctor*, Luke, notes that Jesus was empowered with *divine* help from the Holy Spirit. He went about doing good-i.e., healing all, revealing *disease* is not good and not God. He reveals that sick people were oppressed by the *devil*. There is an integration of different factors, all to the end that people are healed. It is important not to separate one factor and make it the sole focus of healing. I made this serious mistake once upon a time.

"Throw Out All Your Meds!"

"You must throw out all your medications, cancel your health insurance and never step foot in a doctor's office again," the prominent Bible teacher admonished. "These are the absolute conditions if you ever want to receive healing from God. He does not tolerate any help from the 'arm of the flesh.' Cursed is the person who trusts man. There can be no mix of medicine, man and God." Crazy? Somewhat. Dangerous? Possibly. God's heart? No! Quite a significant number of unwarranted and needless deaths have occurred in groups that adhere to this strict teaching of separation between God's ways of healing and man's ways. I should know. For a brief time, many years ago, my husband and I listened to this teacher and embraced some of his teachings. While we learned some important things about God's desire to heal, we were filled with fear and misled about God's love, compassion and His blessing of "the arm of the flesh" or medical help. Then, thanks to the Holy Spirit, we were redirected on the biblical path of healing, a path that is not dualistic in nature, separating the spiritual, supernatural from the natural, physical. We recognized that God's blessing and healing often come through man, medicine and the entire medical community. We are very thankful for all the medical advances in curing diseases. We are grateful to the dedicated men and women who practice medicine. Can people put too much trust in medical doctors and medicines? Of course. That is why we teach people to see the whole picture of healing, including all factors as they make decisions about their specific condition. Our Father wants us well and He is teaching us how to wisely cooperate with Him—miraculously, medically, naturally and supernaturally. He is the best doctor. Let's listen to Him. History itself reveals that all of these factors—disease, the devil, divine help and doctors—have been involved in healing for a very long time as people have made decisions about how to get well.

> Our Father wants us well and He is teaching us how to wisely cooperate with Him—miraculously, medically, naturally and supernaturally. He is the best doctor.

Healing History

A brief look at the history of healing is quite fascinating. According to Alex Loyd, co-author of The Healing Codes, there were five eras of healing. The first era was prayer. Before human beings knew or understood nutrition or any type of medicine, all they could do was pray. Early accounts in the Bible show Abraham praying to God for healing.

> Then Abraham prayed to God, and God healed Abimelech, and also healed his wife and female slaves so that they bore children. Genesis 20:17 ESV

History is full of accounts of people looking to various deities for healing through rituals, idolatry or religious practices of all types. People were often aware of the battle between good and evil and they sought to appease the "god of good" in order to be free from the "god of evil." Prayer continues to this day, including all types, both Christian and non-Christian. The second era of healing involved the discovery of the healing properties of leaves, twigs, roots and bark. This began a long history of herb use that has been more popular in the Eastern hemisphere, but has recently gained more attention and use in the West. Western civilization has expanded this emphasis to include a large vitamin/nutritional industry (see Loyd, p. 35). The third era of healing was drug and chemical advances. Big Pharma, the derogatory catch-all name for the huge pharmaceutical industry, continues to dominate treatment of sickness and disease in America. While many drugs have been used to successfully treat disease, the astronomical cost and serious side effects of these drugs hinder their effectiveness. Surgery was the fourth era, although people dabbled in primitive surgery for years even before the discovery of anesthesia. As Loyd states, "While statistics indicate a significant number of surgeries are performed unnecessarily, surgical trauma medicine has been a great gift to civilization and is responsible for saving countless lives (p.38). The final frontier in healing is the current exploration of energy. While much has yet to be learned in this arena, I do think it is interesting that experts are recognizing the importance of energy in the body and how it integrates with our God-given immune system. God is at work now as He has been in the past to bring healing to His creation. Once again, there are a number of factors to consider when we approach healing, but we can be assured that God is in the middle, bringing fresh discoveries and insight so His children can receive healing for themselves and pass on to others. I think we have exciting days ahead! And we have the best doctor on our team.

> Once again, there are a number of factors to consider when we approach healing, but we can be assured that God is in the middle, bringing fresh discoveries and insight so His children can receive healing for themselves and pass on to others.

No Formulas

Learning to trust Jesus as the best doctor does not happen overnight.

There is no formula to follow. It takes time to develop a relationship of faith. We will look at that more fully in Chapter 3. Although we made many mistakes through the years, my husband and I made a decision early on to trust Jesus as the best doctor for our family. That proved to be quite a challenge raising four active sons and an athletic daughter. But it also proved, beyond a shadow of a doubt, that Jesus IS the best doctor, a faithful physician who loves us deeply and is ready to guide us to experience a healthy life. One commitment we made was to always go to Jesus first whenever anyone in our family had a healing need. That meant we prayed first, listened for God's wisdom and direction and sometimes waited before we rushed off to do something. This resulted, for our family, in no one ever needing any antibiotics while growing to adulthood. With recent research showing just how damaging widespread prescription of antibiotics has been, we are grateful for that gift. This, in no way, is meant to condemn those who have used antibiotics, but is just an illustration of how we experienced Jesus as the best doctor for our family. Of course, our children had stitches for open wounds, casts for broken bones, surgery for torn tendons, oatmeal baths for chicken pox and lots of calamine lotion for poison ivy and poison oak. Together with good food, adequate sleep, plenty of fresh air, sunshine and exercise to boot, their bodies grew strong and healthy as God designed them to be. There are still many opportunities to trust Jesus as the best doctor and listen for His help in each situation, and I know there will be many more. But one thing remains unchanged. I still pray God's Word over our family (now numbering 28 and counting) every day.

Bless the LORD, O my soul,
and all that is within me,
bless His holy name!
Bless the LORD, O my soul,
and forget not all His benefits,
who forgives all your iniquity,
who heals all your diseases,
who redeems your life from the pit,
who crowns you with steadfast love and mercy,
who satisfies you with good
so that your youth is renewed like the eagle's. Psalm 103:1-5 ESV

I choose to look to Jesus first. He is the best doctor. He knows me best. He knows you best. Every person has a history and a life situation that bring specific and unique challenges in regard to healing. Some of you face overwhelming physical odds. Others of you have family members who are suffering. But I want to encourage you to start now. Ask the Holy Spirit to reveal to you that Jesus is the best doctor. Begin to saturate yourself in reading the Gospels of Matthew, Mark, Luke and John where Jesus heals all kinds of people with all kinds of disease and afflictions. See how Jesus moved with compassion and power to make people well. That is His will for you, too. Begin to listen for His next steps for you. These are decisions you can make today.

Discussion Questions

1. What are your thoughts and feelings when you hear these phrases:
   a. "Jesus heals today."
   b. "God wants everyone well."
   c. "His will is healing."
2. How have you seen or experienced Jesus working, both medically and miraculously?
3. What have you thought was the cause of sickness and disease? How has this affected your view of healing?

Jesus Conquered Sickness

An Unlikely Meeting

As part of my job, I occasionally travel to teach and train others how to cooperate with Jesus in order to release His healing today. A few years ago while waiting for a flight connection, I had some time to kill. I felt led to take a chance sharing the love of Jesus with the people around me.

I was seated next to a Chinese gentleman. I believed the Lord was indicating to me that this man had a back problem. Situations like this are interesting because you never quite know how things are going to turn out. I decided to take a risk and asked the man if he had any problems with his back. Confused, he looked at me and told me that he didn't (Oh, man!!). He then asked why I wanted to know. I told him that if he did, I would love to pray and that we may see Jesus show up and heal him. The man sat back in his seat and made it clear he was tuning me out.

No sooner did he sit back, than the Chinese woman sitting next to him leaned forward and excitedly started a conversation with me. She inquired about praying for people for healing and where I attend church. After a series of questions, she clarified:

"Are you headed to Champaign too?"

"Yes," I replied, "that's home for me."

"Alright. Would you be willing to come and pray for my father with me? I'm headed home because he's dying of cancer."

"Absolutely. Is this your first time out visiting him?"

"I don't get to see him much. My husband is actually Billy Graham's son, so we're pretty busy with ministry. My father has been a professor at the university in town there for a number of years."

"WAIT...did you just say what I thought you said?!?! Billy Graham is your father-in-law??"

"Yeah," she continued, "as I said, we're pretty busy. Will you be able to come and pray for my father?"

We exchanged contact information and I ruminated on what just happened. How did I miss a word of knowledge and wind up meeting Billy Graham's daughter-in-law? What on earth was God doing here?

When It Doesn't Happen...

A few days later I nervously met my new friend at her father's house. Her father was on a hospital bed at his home. I took one look at him and could tell why his daughter had come to see him; the prognosis must have been a short timeline.

After hearing a bit about the condition I prayed my best prayer for healing, but it didn't take. His health kept spiraling downward and he passed away not too long after that prayer session.

I was confused; wasn't God creating this unlikely connection? Why then didn't we see the cancer destroyed and healing come? And how do I process that? Did I mess up, or is God just toying with me?

This is the reason why the subject of healing is so difficult for us. Each of us has a relative, friend or loved one that we were or are emotionally invested in for their healing. We want to hold out hope, but what if it doesn't happen? In some ways it is easier to just cross the subject off all together. If we don't open ourselves to believe Jesus does still heal today, we don't have to ask what is going on when people don't get healed.

This is where the rubber hits the road in our journey of faith, and how we wrestle through this has everything to do with how we live our faith out every day.

This is where the rubber hits the road in our journey of faith, and how we wrestle through this has everything to do with how we live our faith out every day.

Why Does What Happens, Happen?

Let's back up a bit and ask a slightly more general question. When we ask why someone is or is not healed, we are asking about a specific instance of a more general question: What exactly determines which events happen? In this vast and intricate creation, what dynamics are involved with causality, and how is God wrapped up in that?

Before you tune out the rest of the chapter because this may be getting too philosophical, let me assure you we won't drift off into metaphysics. I'll keep this accessible.

There are essentially two options on the table to consider; either the universe is running according to a **cosmic blueprint**, or it is caught up in a **cosmic war**. Which of these we embrace makes all the difference in how we understand God, how we see ourselves and what the life of faith looks like.

A Masterful Designer

The cosmic blueprint perspective sees God as the supreme designer. He is the divine mechanic and designer that has carefully coordinated and calibrated the whole of the universe to do exactly what He foresaw before He created all things. The world, our lives, all of time has been blueprinted in advance and is rolling out according to God's design.

The core idea in this perspective is rulership. God is the ultimate king, and as such, His rule extends unanimously over every aspect of creation. What God has designed to happen will happen, and it's as simple as that. Whatever we do or don't understand about our lives, we can rest assured on this fundamental premise: God is orchestrating it all.

The cosmic blueprint perspective is revealed in phrases that we use to process life at times, "Everything happens for a reason." (Implication: God is driving all events.) Or, "God works in mysterious ways." (Implication: We may not understand God's will, but we know that what is happening is God's will.)

This last phrase captures the role of the believer in this perspective. Since we know God's will is always happening, our primary intersection with God's will is one of reconciling ourselves to be at peace with what comes into our lives. We may or may not like what happens at first, but we can learn to embrace it as God's plan for our life and find God within it. God's sovereignty starts to become a primary connection point for how we think of Him, and we see our lives and the world around us as living out God's predestined plan.

An Invading General

The cosmic war perspective approaches the whole question differently. Rather than seeing this world as living out a pre-planned design, this perspective portrays our world as the front lines of an invisible spiritual battlefield. The forces of light and darkness are clashing, and the battlelines are drawn through our lives.

While the cosmic blueprint may assert the same premise that good and evil are in a battle, the cosmic war perspective takes that thought a step further and says that battle is a battle of two legitimate free wills. While we know at the end of the day Jesus is victorious, how exactly we get to that victory hasn't been fully predetermined. The devil and his minions are free agents that at times frustrate God's will. In other words, God's will does not always happen.

God's will, in fact, is exactly what that battle is all about. When the side of light wins, God's will is done in whatever area that battle was over. When the side of darkness is victorious, God's will doesn't happen in that place. The world is a cosmic struggle for the forces of the kingdom of God to overthrow the strongholds of the enemy and enforce God's will.

The role of the believer in this paradigm is altogether different than in the cosmic blueprint perspective. The impetus on believers is that we've been drafted into the fight. We are a part of the Lord's army, destroying the works of the devil and releasing the rule of God on this earth. We are not to passively accept the tragedies or challenges of life; rather, we discern whether the enemy is behind them and if so, we work with the Lord to be a part of that battle in this cosmic war.

Choose Your Tension

The cosmic blueprint and cosmic war perspectives each give you a different anchor point for how you understand God. Essentially, these are two different ways to resolve the age-old problem of evil: "If God is all-good and all-powerful, then why is the world falling apart?"

This question essentially pits two of God's attributes against each other: God's goodness (God only wants good things to happen, He does not desire evil), and God's sovereignty (God is the ultimate ruler of the universe. There is no one more supreme than He). Because our world is clearly fallen and broken, we are forced to anchor our understanding of God on one of these two principles and hold the other a little more loosely.

With the cosmic blueprint perspective, the anchor point is God's sovereignty. We may not understand how the situation we're facing right now is connected to God's goodness. It certainly does not seem good when horrible things happen to good people, or when tragedy unexpectedly strikes, but we know God is in control. Someday we will understand how this is God's goodness, but we can trust that God is orchestrating this now.

In the cosmic war perspective, the anchor point is God's goodness, and His sovereignty seems more abstract. We evaluate each situation through the lens of the kingdom by which it comes to us, knowing that

Jesus is bringing us life and the enemy is the one who causes death. We can trust and depend on God's goodness; He isn't sending bad things into our lives, but He is always the force of redemption for what the enemy causes. The tension on this side is reconciling God's sovereignty. If God is in charge, why does the enemy seem to get his way so often? And why, when we fight the battle, don't we always win? Aren't we on the victorious side?

Each side has strengths and each side has a tension. In order to live out our Christian faith though, we have to choose a side. We cannot relate to God on the backdrop of the events of our lives without landing somewhere on this question.

What Does Jesus Look Like?

People on both sides of these choices will argue from Scripture for the validity for their perspective. Ironically, the very same verses can be argued on both sides because words carry different meanings in each perspective (a good example is the way the word "predestined" is interpreted in each point of view). Each side can give chapter and verse to defend its validity, but what is really happening is theologians are reading their perspective into Scripture. How do we decide how to approach this issue?

The safest way to proceed is to look at Jesus. Here is an important maxim to keep in mind: Jesus is the clearest picture of God there is. When we are trying to understand who God is, sometimes things can be confusing; it can seem like we see one picture of God in the Old Testament and something completely separate in Jesus in the New Testament. Which picture are we to look to?

> Jesus is the clearest picture of God there is.

The New Testament repeatedly highlights that Jesus is where God comes into clarity. Whenever we aren't sure how to understand God, we need to come back to the person of Jesus.

Long ago, at many times and in many ways, God spoke to our fathers by the prophets, but in these last days he has spoken to us by his Son, whom he appointed the heir of all things, through whom also he created the world. He is the radiance of the glory of God and the exact imprint of his nature, and he upholds the universe by the word of his power. Hebrews 1:1-3 ESV

Notice the very first verses the writer pens to the Hebrews (the audience most familiar with the Old Testament): God did speak by the prophets, God has spoken before and He is present in the Old Testament. But after that, He spoke by His Son, who is the exact imprint of His nature. Jesus is the clear picture of God.

This theme is present throughout the New Testament; Jesus is what God looks like. (See John 1:17-18, Matthew 17:1-8, John 14:9 and Colossians 2:9 for a few more examples.)

The relevant question for us, then, is this: "Does Jesus demonstrate living by the cosmic blueprint or the cosmic war?" If we really can look at Jesus and see the Father, then we should be able to see the answer to this question by looking at Him. With that, let's consider two passages.

The first is a response Jesus gives when two of His disciples try to preempt the others and get the most favored seats in Jesus' coming kingdom. Jesus uses this as a teaching moment for all His disciples:

But Jesus called them to him and said, "You know that the rulers of the Gentiles lord it over them, and their great ones exercise authority over them. It shall not be so among you. But whoever would be great among you must be your servant, and whoever would be first among you must be your slave, even as the Son of Man came not to be served but to serve, and to give his life as a ransom for many." Matthew 20:25-28 ESV

Notice what Jesus is arguing here. The rulers of the Gentiles lord their authority over others. They exercise their authority constantly—forcing their will, micromanaging the people they have charge over. They are approving and checking every choice, retaining control. Jesus says that it is not to be like that with the disciples because that is not how He behaves. Rather, Jesus says that He uses His authority to serve, not to impose.

I would suggest to you that if Jesus really is the picture of the Father, this means we cannot live in a cosmic blueprint. A cosmic blueprint is a world where God's greatness is measured by His control; by the fact that He does constantly exercise his authority. God's will always happens; everything else is thrown out! Yet, that is exactly what Jesus says is not the way He uses His authority.

Speaking of His goodness, here is what Jesus says:

The thief comes only to steal and kill and destroy. I came that they may have life and have it abundantly. John 10:10 ESV

Jesus makes a clear distinction. He is purely and simply on the side of good, and destruction comes from the enemy. 1 John echoes this sentiment:

This is the message we have heard from him and proclaim to you, that God is light, and in him is no darkness at all. 1 John 1:5 ESV

This is John's summary of what Jesus communicated: that God is light and in Him is no darkness. God isn't playing both sides. He is not causing good and evil. He is only on the side of goodness. The evil that happens in this world has nothing to do with God, it is what God is acting against.

Finding Our Footing All Over Again

For the rest of this book, we will approach healing through the perspective of the cosmic war perspective. This is a sentiment that is foreign to many. The default assumption for much of the church (indeed, even culture outside the church) is that our universe is a cosmic blueprint, but that is not what we see highlighted in the person of Jesus.

If you're adopting this perspective for the first time, it likely means we need to go back and rethink many things. If you were to get up and walk to the opposite side of the room you're in now, your point of view on every single object in the room would change. To change your perspective means you have to reexamine everything. That will indeed be a part of our journey.

Specifically, let's look at how the cosmic war perspective informs our understanding of healing. What is happening when someone gets healed? How do we think about it when healing doesn't happen?

Recall our anchor point from before: God is good, and His goodness is simple. It's not a complicated we-will-understand-someday kind of goodness. It is a pure and simple goodness. In the case of healing, this translates into an anchor point we can believe—that health and wholeness is God's will. It is God's will that we are well. God wants our lives to conform to His design, and humanity was designed to be in health. Sickness is a distortion of the way God designed our body to function.

We can take this as a given because we know that in eternity there will be no more sickness:

> *He will wipe away every tear from their eyes, and death shall be no more, neither shall there be mourning, nor crying, nor pain anymore, for the former things have passed away.* Revelation 21:4 ESV

At the end of the story, God removes every form of damage of this creation. Death is removed, pain is banished and tears are but a memory. God's design in our bodies and our hearts is fully realized.

If that is God's ultimate desire in eternity, it is also His desire today. The fallen nature of this world does not change God's heart. God desires for us to be whole and healthy in every dimension of our being. Jesus Christ is the same yesterday, today and forever (Hebrews 13:8) and His will is for our healing.

The way we process when healing does or doesn't happen is then through the context of the battle for our world. When someone is healed, God's will has happened in that portion of someone's life. When we pray for someone and they are not healed, it is because in this situation, God's will has not happened. Why has God's will not happened there? I don't know. The spiritual realm is very complex and we don't often get an answer to that question. What we do know is that Jesus wants them healed and we can continue to partner with Him to hopefully someday see that happen. Even if we don't though, we have the guarantee that someday in eternity we will see complete healing.

Sickness (and disease in general) is a tool that belongs to Satan. As we previously saw, John 10:10 indicates that theft, death and destruction belongs to him. Sickness results in all three of these in our lives; it steals our quality of life, it works to destroy our ability to enjoy this life God has given us, and it may even work to eventually kill us entirely.

Sickness is a tool of Satan's, and one that unfortunately is often one that he has been able to pin back on God. By picking up a cosmic blueprint perspective, the church has absorbed the tools of the enemy back into the will of God. When that happens, sickness becomes a blessing from God that is sent to sanctify us. To be clear, God can and does work through sickness. He is amazing enough that even when the enemy presents his tools, God can work His good in our lives nonetheless. The ends, however, do not justify the means. God may use the stress a marriage goes through because a spouse is addicted to pornography to eventually strengthen the couple, but that does not mean pornography is somehow a blessing from God. Likewise, sickness is not something God sends into our lives to grow us up. If it is present, God will use it, but He is quite capable of growing us up without having to sink to dispatching the tools of Satan on us Himself.

The pattern of sickness being allowed by God to work redemptively was not a theme we see in Jesus' ministry. At no point did He allow someone to remain in sickness because God was using it. At no point did He tell someone their sickness was from the Lord and they needed to bear that burden. No, in every recorded account, Jesus healed the person of their condition. Once again, if Jesus is the clearest picture of the Father, then we have to come to the conclusion that healing is God's will.

> The pattern of sickness being allowed by God to work redemptively was not a theme we see in Jesus' ministry. At no point did He allow someone to remain in sickness because God was using it.

Conquering Sickness

Another anchor point we can cling to is that Jesus is more powerful than sickness. He conquered sickness because He conquered the author of sickness. Jesus coming to earth was God's invasion to take back this planet from the clutches of the evil one. On His way to the cross this is Jesus' statement:

Now is the judgment of this world; now will the ruler of this world be cast out. John 12:31 ESV

Jesus came and He brought His heavenly kingdom with Him. That kingdom is invading this world, binding up the works of darkness and releasing God's will. Light is shining in the darkness and wholeness is overtaking brokenness.

The cross is the ultimate showdown between Jesus and Satan. They climb in the ring and go man-to-serpent with each other, no-holds-barred. Satan leads with some of his classic tools: betrayal, accusation, mockery. Eventually he ups the ante and throws in public humiliation and torture. All of this is leading up to his coup-de-grace–death. Death is Satan's ultimate weapon. It has never failed before–every time a threat to his kingdom has appeared in the past, death has successfully resolved the problem.

All the while, Jesus seems to be just taking it on the chin. He's not fighting back, He's not trying to avoid it, He's just letting it come. This is because God's plan was bigger than the enemy could see. He wasn't wanting to just overpower the enemy, He wanted to disarm him entirely. Isaiah 53 gives us a bit of an insight as to what is happening:

Surely he has borne our griefs/sicknesses
and carried our sorrows/pains;
yet we esteemed him stricken,
smitten by God, and afflicted.
But he was pierced for our transgressions;
he was crushed for our iniquities;
upon him was the chastisement that brought us peace,
and with his wounds we are healed.
All we like sheep have gone astray;
we have turned–every one–to his own way;
and the Lord has laid on him
the iniquity of us all. Isaiah 53:4-6 ESV

In the process leading up to the cross, Jesus was bearing our wounds. All the brokenness of humanity was being laid on Him. This is what the mockery, the beatings, the abuse was about. Jesus was actually entering into our brokenness. It was not about God punishing Him (note lines two and three—Isaiah points out this is a mistaken way to understand these events), it was about Jesus fully entering into the brokenness of fallen humanity. In our sin, in our shame and in our sickness.

When Satan then puts Jesus up on the cross, he is not just murdering a man, he is unknowingly using death to kill sin and sickness. He is using his chief weapon to undermine all his secondary weapons. And then the power of death—even that wasn't powerful enough to defeat Jesus. He stayed in the grave a measly 36 hours.

In His battle with Satan, Jesus proved himself more powerful than the master of sin, sickness and death, and in that, He subjugated those powers to Himself. Jesus is now the master of sickness, it now answers to Him.

The Continuing Story

After the cross, Jesus does something unexpected, He drafts His disciples into the battle. Having overthrown the "ruler of this world," Jesus gives them some final instructions:

> And Jesus came and said to them, "All authority in heaven and on earth has been given to me. Go therefore and make disciples of all nations, baptizing them in the name of the Father and of the Son and of the Holy Spirit, teaching them to observe all that I have commanded you. And behold, I am with you always, to the end of the age." Matthew 28:18-20 ESV

Now that all authority on earth (including authority over sickness) has been given to Jesus, He dispatches His disciples to go everywhere and introduce others to this new life He has modeled and revealed to them.

After defeating the general of the opposing forces, Jesus passes the baton to the church. He could have snapped His fingers and finished the fight Himself, but that would have violated the original design, which was to release His rule on earth through partnership with humanity (Genesis 1:28).

The Church has been given the marching orders to continue to enforce the victory of Jesus. He has overthrown the power of sickness. It is now subjugated to Him. We come along and enforce that victory. We get to co-rule with Jesus by overthrowing the works of the enemy.

Jesus conquered sickness. All sickness has not yet been banished, but the power to overthrow sickness has been given to you and me. It is time for the church to rise up and step into the place of authority that Jesus has given us. As we do, we will see Jesus heal today.

Discussion Questions

1. Have you seen the world through the cosmic blueprint or the cosmic war perspective? How has that affected the way you've processed healing?

2. Read the story found in Mark 9:20-29. Discuss the battle we see happening in this passage. What do you think is the main point of this story?

3. Share your reaction to the statement: "Healing can definitely be a process, so it is important not to give up."

Chapter **3**

Jesus Honors Faith

A Desperate and Daring Faith

Rhoda had been in tremendous pain for twelve long years due to constant bleeding. This had destroyed her ability to have a normal life of marriage, intimacy, children, even work and friendship. She, of course, sought help from several different doctors. Many gladly took her money and some even took her dignity, but all failed to bring her healing. Ultimately, her physical condition worsened right along with her sense of despair. She was resigned to a life of battling weakness, pain and hopelessness. Then she heard there was a new doctor in town who was having some success with different illnesses. In spite of her extreme fatigue and her history of failed attempts, she decided to see what he could do. Twenty-four hours later, she returned home, not just feeling a little bit better, but 100% healed—no more bleeding, weakness, pain—healthy and whole for the first time in twelve years! What happened? What did this doctor do that others couldn't? Who was this doctor?

This doctor was Jesus. He did what no other doctor had been able to do for her. She was made well! This story, with which I have taken some liberty, is nevertheless recorded for us in Mark 5 and provides valuable insight into receiving healing from Jesus.

> And there was a woman who had had a discharge of blood for twelve years, and who had suffered much under many physicians, and had spent all that she had, and was no better but rather grew worse. She had heard the reports about Jesus and came up behind him in the crowd and touched his garment. For she said, "If I touch even his garments, I will be made well." And immediately the flow of blood dried up, and she felt in her body that she was healed of her disease. And Jesus, perceiving in himself that power had gone out from him, immediately turned about in the crowd and said, "Who touched my garments?" And his disciples said to him, "You see the crowd pressing around you, and yet you say, 'Who touched me?'" And he looked around to see who had done it. But the woman, knowing what had happened to her, came in fear and trembling and fell down before him and told him the whole truth. And he said to her, "Daughter, your faith has made you well; go in peace, and be healed of your disease."
> Mark 5:25-34 ESV

Jesus' commendation to her, "Daughter, your faith has made you well," highlights the importance of faith in receiving healing from Jesus. Her faith was especially profound given her weakened condition, her many years of failed attempts at healing, her outright disobedience to Jewish Law(which would have forbidden her to be in public with bloody discharge that defiled others) and as a woman, she would not have been allowed to travel without a male escort. She did not let any of those obstacles stop her from getting to Jesus. Was she afraid? Yes, trembling! Was she unsure? Absolutely! Was this difficult? No doubt! This conflicts with those who say you cannot have fear, doubt, or complications when it comes to the faith that Jesus honors. This woman reflects quite a different picture of faith—a desperate, yet daring faith. This should encourage all of us who struggle with doubt and fear. Jesus honors "imperfect" faith.

This woman reflects quite a different picture of faith—a desperate, yet daring faith. This should encourage all of us who struggle with doubt and fear. Jesus honors "imperfect" faith.

By no means is the above account an isolated incidence of Jesus noting a person's faith for healing. There are a number of stories where Jesus specifically points to faith as a key element for healing. There is no question, when it comes to healing, that Jesus honors faith, delights in faith, responds to faith and encourages faith. Therefore, it is imperative that we discover what Jesus means by faith and how we can flow in faith today to receive the healings we need for ourselves and others.

To be clear, not all healing Jesus did involved a specific mention of faith. There were numbers of mass healings where faith is not referenced. There are also individual healings that do not specify faith as a factor. Yet, faith is prominent in Jesus' healing ministry. Let's discover more about this powerful element of faith that Jesus says actually moves mountains and uproots trees.

> And Jesus answered them, "Have faith in God. Truly, I say to you, whoever says to this mountain, 'Be taken up and thrown into the sea,' and does not doubt in his heart, but believes that what he says will come to pass, it will be done for him. Therefore I tell you, whatever you ask in prayer, believe that you have received it, and it will be yours." Mark 11:22-24 ESV

Jesus tells us that faith accomplishes the impossible, even bringing healing to those who are desperate and have tried everything else to be made well. Have faith in God! Sounds simple, but...there is quite a bit of confusion today concerning faith for healing. In part, the confusion is due to inaccurate and, at times, even harmful teaching that is present in the church. In addition, some people are not aware of what biblical faith is and how to receive and move in faith for healing. Then, too, there are the two Kingdoms in conflict (see Chapter 2) which means there is at times a real battle for healing and answers do not come easily. In light of these dilemmas, it is important to not only know what faith is, but also to know what faith is not.

Faith Is Not...

"I can't figure out why I am still sick," said the bewildered man as he shook his head. "After all, I have faith. I really do believe. I believe healing is for today. I believe Jesus wants to heal me. I believe I have done everything I can—receive medical help, receive prayer, and I have even fasted. I believe I should get better, but I can't seem to be free of these menacing migraines. I thought believing brought healing." I know there are many who can identify with this man's confusion in regards to faith and believing. I have heard this same comment over and over. It is a common sentiment to lament, "I believe, but nothing seems to change." What is the problem? What should one do? It is not wise nor helpful to respond, "Believe more or believe harder!"

Faith is not just believing with our mind that healing is for today or that Jesus wants to heal you today. Such believing is a good start and is definitely more truth than many have believed throughout history. However, faith is not just intellectual agreement with these truths. James tells us "even the demons believe" (James 2:19). But biblical faith is not just a head exercise. Biblical faith is of the heart. At its core, faith is childlike trust in God Himself (more on this later). It will suffice for now to know the faith that Jesus honors for healing is not just believing something is true and mentally acquiescing with that truth, as important as that is. Faith is not a mere statement of the facts nor is faith something that is needed in great quantities, contrary to what some people teach.

> Faith is not just believing with our mind that healing is for today or that Jesus wants to heal you today. Such believing is a good start and is definitely more truth than many have believed throughout history. However, faith is not just intellectual agreement with these truths.

"You do not have enough faith!" the authoritarian voice of the pastor announced to the weeping mother as she stood helplessly before him. She wrapped her arms tighter around her bundled baby, whose refusal to eat had baffled the doctors and frightened this new mother. "If you had faith, your baby would be well. Meet the conditions of faith, then healing will come." Filled with fear, the mother was desperate for God to show her how she could produce enough faith to bring healing to her baby.

Bring healing? That sounds more like "buy" healing! This teaching is twisted at best, tragic at worst. This is not faith as Jesus taught nor is it the faith that Jesus commended. Yet this is the faith that some teachers and pastors in the Body of Christ demand people to produce. While this "hyper-faith" is more the extreme and the exception, it is still taught and has destroyed innocent lives. Many people have even lost faith in God altogether after they were blamed for not having enough faith to be healed. No, faith is not a commodity one can produce enough of to please God and thus compel Him to heal. That is not biblical faith. Pagans try to appease false gods. Christians trust the living, loving true God.

Jesus never told anyone they needed more faith or condemned them for failure to get well because they lacked faith. He did rebuke His own disciples for not having faith to heal an epileptic boy oppressed by a demon.

> And when they had come to the multitude, a man came to Him, kneeling down to Him and saying, "Lord, have mercy on my son, for he is an epileptic and suffers severely; for he often falls into the fire and often into the water. So I brought him to Your disciples, but they could not cure him." Then Jesus answered and said, "O faithless and perverse generation, how long shall I be with you? How long shall I bear with you? Bring him here to Me." And Jesus rebuked the demon, and it came out of him; and the child was cured from that very hour. Then the disciples came to Jesus privately and said, "Why could we not cast it out?" So Jesus said to them, "Because of your unbelief; for assuredly, I say to you, if you have faith as a mustard seed, you will say to this mountain, 'Move from here to there,' and it will move; and nothing will be impossible for you." Matthew 17:14-20 NKJV

Obviously, quantity is not the issue when it comes to faith since a mustard seed size, one of the smallest seeds, is all that is needed to move a mountain. For those preachers, teachers who have perhaps blamed others for their lack of faith, I, as a teacher, would say, "Let's look at our own faith as we pray for others. Maybe we lack faith, not the one who is sick." This is sobering for all of us who are committed to praying for others. Believers are sent to heal the sick. Jesus said:

> *"And these signs will follow those who believe: In My name they will cast out demons;.... they will lay hands on the sick, and they will recover." Mark 16:17, 18b ESV*

Jesus wants us believers to be able to lay hands on the sick and see them recover. We don't rebuke the sick for their unbelief. We release faith for their healing and get to rejoice as they recover. I, for one, want to experience this more. Teach us Lord, so we may have faith to heal the sick. We now know that faith is not about quantity. Faith is also not about denying the facts.

> Jesus wants us believers to be able to lay hands on the sick and see them recover. We don't rebuke the sick for their unbelief. We release faith for their healing and get to rejoice as they recover.

"I know you got a bad report from the oncologist," the Bible teacher sympathized, "but just believe in your heart and confess with your mouth every day, 'I am healed. I do not have cancer.' Only say positive things about your condition and never agree with the doctor's diagnosis. This is true faith." While saying positive things about one's health can be a helpful practice, this is not the essence of biblical faith for healing. The faith that Jesus honors for healing is not dependent on a person denying the actual diagnosis of disease. There is no magic in positively repeating something that is not true in an attempt to change it. This has been a popular "faith" teaching where people were encouraged to "name it, claim it," in an attempt to be healed. Again, while positive thinking and speaking positively have benefits, they are not what faith is.

To receive healing from Jesus and have a faith that He honors, you do not have to be super spiritual, a certain race or gender or a put-together perfectionist. That is good news for all of us! No matter how insignificant or unqualified we may feel, we can choose to have faith in Jesus and go to Him.

All of these illustrations are based on true stories of real people and all of them confirm the fact that there is much confusion today in regards to faith for healing. I could share other misconceptions about faith for healing, but I think these make the point. Because it is so obvious from Scripture that Jesus honors faith when it comes to healing, people have earnestly tried to figure out what true faith is. We do not have all the answers by any means, but we do know the Holy Spirit is eager to teach us truth to set us free. The Bible has some interesting clues about the presence and practice of faith as shown by those who came to Jesus for healing. We will examine different interactions of Jesus with some of these individuals and attempt to discover a clear picture of the faith Jesus honors. What is so fascinating is that all of these people are quite ordinary people—a blind beggar, a desperate mother who was not a Jew and not qualified to receive Israel's blessing for her demonized daughter, a Roman soldier who came for his dying servant, a group of crazy friends who tore off a roof for their paralyzed comrade, and an ostracized leper in defiance of Jewish laws of isolation. The point is: To receive healing from Jesus and have a faith that He honors, you do not have to be super spiritual, a certain race or gender or a put-together perfectionist. That is good news for all of us! No matter how insignificant or unqualified we may feel, we can choose to have faith in Jesus and go to Him.

Presence of Jesus

Go to Him? Yes. In all of the stories we'll examine, there are many variables, but there is one unchangeable factor in every healing story where Jesus commends the person's faith. Each person got in the presence of Jesus. So, you might say, "That's great for them, but Jesus is no longer on earth, so how does this relate to my situation? I can't access the presence of Jesus." I understand!

In 1975 when I was in the throes of a devastating crisis of infertility, I became aware of how much the Bible talks about Jesus as a Healer. I had never been taught this in all my years growing up in the church despite the fact I had read many of His healing accounts. I had relegated such miracles to the first century when Jesus actually walked on earth. As the medical prognosis turned bleak, I became consumed with reading about Jesus' healing and an anguished cry rose up in me: "If only Jesus were here today, I know He would heal me!" I knew if I could just get in His presence, I would be healed. Little did I know, Jesus is here! His presence is here on earth. Yes, that was Jesus' promise to us before He ascended to heaven.

> And I will ask the Father, and he will give you another Helper, to be with you forever, even the Spirit of truth, whom the world cannot receive, because it neither sees him nor knows him. You know him, for he dwells with you and will be in you. "I will not leave you as orphans; I will come to you. Yet a little while and the world will see me no more, but you will see me. Because I live, you also will live. In that day you will know that I am in my Father, and you in me, and I in you. John 14:16-20 ESV

We are carriers of God's Presence and that means we carry His healing for ourselves and for others. Being aware of the Holy Spirit and being filled with His presence is vital to having faith for healing today.

We have the privilege of having the Spirit of Christ, the Holy Spirit, live inside of us. We are not left as orphans. We have God Himself, right here, right now, right inside of us. We are carriers of God's Presence and that means we carry His healing for ourselves and for others. Being aware of the Holy Spirit and being filled with His presence is vital to having faith for healing today. When I encountered the Holy Spirit, everything changed for me and eventually led to my receiving faith for healing and the gift of five children.

Since the Holy Spirit is so important, we recommend a whole book on how to know and be filled with the Holy Spirit in the conclusion. We no longer have to say, "If only Jesus were here" because Jesus is here. By His Spirit, He gives us the faith we need to live in health. And Jesus is still healing the sick through us, His Body on earth, who are filled with His Holy Spirit and have faith to obey Him. So, in light of what we have now learned, we ask: "What exactly is faith?"

Faith Is...

According to the writer of Hebrews,

> Now faith is the assurance of things hoped for, the conviction of things not seen. Hebrews 11:1 ESV

In regards to healing...faith means we are assured in our heart that what we hope for (healing) is ours and we are strong in our conviction of this even though we don't yet see or experience the healing we need. Faith is needed only when we do not visibly possess what we want. But—and this is a very big but—our faith is actually in the person of Jesus, His promise to heal, His power to heal, His desire to heal. Our faith is not some abstract force or attitude or energy we conjure up. Our faith is simple, childlike trust in Jesus Himself. Thus, He is both the Author or originator of our faith and also the Perfecter or finisher of our faith—the one who works in us both to will and do His good pleasure (Philippians 2:13).

> Fixing our eyes on Jesus, the Author and Perfecter of faith
> Hebrews 12:2a NASB

Our faith is in Jesus and is lived out in many different ways, depending on the specific situation. Each person can be assured of Jesus' unfailing love and can look to Him for help, faith and healing.

> Our faith is not some abstract force or attitude or energy we conjure up. Our faith is simple, childlike trust in Jesus Himself.

What can we learn from those persons that Jesus noted had faith for healing as they were in His presence? We will see that faith has many faces and is not a formula. Faith, as demonstrated by these people, varies. Different ones demonstrate different aspects of faith in Jesus—faith in Jesus' authority, faith in His goodness and mercy, faith in His identity and faith in His will. Every person has a different dilemma of faith. The important thing to remember is that Jesus is eager for each of us to be filled with faith in Him, no matter our condition or situation. We can learn from these biblical men and women and know Jesus truly honors faith that is expressed in multiple ways.

Faith in Jesus' Authority Despite a War

"I know we have a real enemy, Satan, and I spend time each day binding him up, praying against his work in my life and family, doing warfare so we don't get sick or have trouble," the serious-faced mother shared with me. First, I am pleased that she, unlike others, does recognize that Satan is a real being with real power. Peter tells us:

> Be sober-minded; be watchful. Your adversary the devil prowls around like a roaring lion, seeking someone to devour. Resist him, firm in your faith, knowing that the same kinds of suffering are being experienced by your brotherhood throughout the world. 1 Peter 5:8-8 ESV

Yes, we want to be firm in our faith and resist the devil. We do live in an "already-not yet" tension of the Kingdom of God where the devil, while defeated, is not yet cast into the final lake of fire. (Revelation 20:10) However, it is just as important to recognize and understand the authority Jesus has over Satan. Being Savior-focused and not Satan-focused can make a big difference in the flow of our faith. If we are not settled that the risen King Jesus indeed has all authority in heaven and on earth, we may default to thinking there is an equal battle between Jesus and the devil that is still going on. This is very unsettling to our faith. This can easily destroy our faith. Yes, there is a war, but we fight FROM a place of Jesus' victory over the devil, not FOR it. We believe Jesus has defeated the enemy and that includes sickness and disease.

However, it is just as important to recognize and understand the authority Jesus has over Satan. Being Savior-focused and not Satan-focused can make a big difference in the flow of our faith.

That evening they brought to him many who were oppressed by demons, and he cast out the spirits with a word and healed all who were sick. This was to fulfill what was spoken by the prophet Isaiah: "He took our illnesses and bore our diseases." Matthew 8:16-17 ESV

Jesus has all authority in the Kingdom. When we have faith in His authority, we are strengthened to receive healing for ourselves and others. That is exactly what happened in the life of the Roman centurion and his servant who was dying. This centurion understood authority and recognized the authority Jesus had over a terrible, paralyzing sickness.

When he had entered Capernaum, a centurion came forward to him, appealing to him, "Lord, my servant is lying paralyzed at home, suffering terribly." And he said to him, "I will come and heal him." But the centurion replied, "Lord, I am not worthy to have you come under my roof, but only say the word, and my servant will be healed. For I too am a man under authority, with soldiers under me. And I say to one, 'Go,' and he goes, and to another, 'Come,' and he comes, and to my servant,'Do this,' and he does it." When Jesus heard this, he marveled and said to those who followed him, "Truly, I tell you, with no one in Israel have I found such faith. ..... And to the centurion Jesus said, "Go; let it be done for you as you have believed." And the servant was healed at that very moment. Matthew 8:5-13 ESV

This man understood Jesus' authority. He knew, " Just say the word and my servant will be healed." Yes! That is the power of Jesus' authority. He simply speaks and it is done. That is the same authority He gives to us, His disciples, as we are sent in His Name, in His authority and in the power of His Spirit. We go in His authority and His Name with the full assurance that Jesus has defeated the evil one and Jesus alone is King. We are humbled to be trusted with the Name of Jesus.

At one of our church services, our youth pastor Brandon Henderson prayed for a friend with Jesus' authority. Here is his first person account:

> Yesterday after the 11am service I got to pray for a friend of mine whom I've known for years. She wanted prayer because she was having a procedure done to remove cancerous cell from her cervix. We prayed for healing and **I rebuked the cancerous cell** and took a major risk and told her, "I see them going in to do the procedure, but then saying we can't find anything." She said that she felt the Holy Spirit saying the same thing. She went in for her procedure today and this is what she had to say, "Brandon, I just finished with the procedure and when the doctor put on the solution to find the previous concerning areas, she was shocked and said that my cervix looked "stone cold normal." We went back-and-forth a little bit and whether not I should have the procedure, but she insisted that I continue in order to "biopsy my newly normal looking cervix." I have all faith and give all glory to God.

Note that Brandon "rebuked the cancerous cell." In other words, he took authority by speaking a word in Jesus' powerful name. Faith in Jesus' authority brings healing results. We do not have to be intimidated by the devil. We do not have to be consumed with "fighting" him. No, just have faith in Jesus' authority over all sickness, over all works of the evil one.

Faith in Jesus' Goodness and Mercy Despite Obstacles

It is easy to get discouraged when prayers for healing are not answered—time and time again. It is tempting to doubt God's mercy and His goodness, especially when circumstances and medical reports are negative. We assume Jesus is not really willing to heal this issue and finally, we just give up. Our faith is crushed by the crisis. But faith is for the unseen, even if the crisis has intensified. Faith in Jesus' mercy and goodness means we trust He is faithful to heal and we can trust His mercy will prevail.

When circumstances looked worse than ever, Ed and Kara, a young couple from our church community, chose to worship Jesus and trust Him. It took faith in Jesus' goodness and mercy for Kara and Ed to experience healing, but it was definitely worth it! Kara writes:

We received a phone call from our OB doctor notifying us that our pregnancy labs were decreasing and we were facing our third miscarriage. We were devastated. We had been praying for a healthy pregnancy and knew that it was God's desire for us, so why had we been through so much heartache? We began to doubt God and His promise. We knew that after a third miscarriage we would medically qualify to see a fertility specialist. It seemed like the right answer to help our heartache. We told our OB doctor to start the referral process. As soon as we hung up the phone with our OB doctor we felt like God was speaking to us in a very intimate way! God kept telling us... "Trust me, I AM the ultimate healer. My desire is for you to have a healthy pregnancy." So we hit our knees and began to pray! God knew the desire of our heart was to be parents and we trusted that He would honor those desires! Sunday morning we went to church and during praise and worship God was revealing Himself in a big way! We could sense the Holy Spirit's presence and I got really warm and shaky and began to weep. I looked up at Ed and said we need to go forward for prayer and healing. As soon as the invitation was given to go forward we ran down to meet Di. We told Di that we had received news that our labs were indicating another miscarriage, but that we kept hearing God's voice through prayer that he was bigger than this. Di laid hands on us and professed that God's desire for us was to have a healthy pregnancy and she prayed for healing over this pregnancy, future pregnancies and my body. We left with confirmation that God was in charge. That Wednesday I did miscarry. I remember thinking, "God what was all that about? You spoke to us in a very real way. If you are the ultimate healer, why didn't you heal this?" Through prayer God just kept saying, "Trust me, I am bigger than any fertility specialist. I am the Ultimate Healer of all things. I do know the desires of your heart, and I am faithful." As hard as it was, we put our trust in His promise.

A few weeks went by and I started having symptoms indicating I was pregnant. We thought there was no way. It was just two weeks prior that we had miscarried. But God kept speaking to our hearts so we decided to take a pregnancy test and it turned positive immediately. We called our OB doctor to share the news and with hesitation she ordered pregnancy labs. Our labs were extremely high and kept climbing, a sign of a healthy pregnancy! We went in a couple of weeks later to see the beautiful site of our baby's heartbeat. We had conceived exactly two weeks after our third miscarriage—something that rarely happens according to medical textbooks and statistics.

Thank God He is bigger than any statistic, medical textbook or fertility specialist. Thank you God for being so real, steadfast after our hearts, and faithful. God did prove that He is the Ultimate Healer!!! On June 2nd 2012 @ 7:09 am the most beautiful creation- Emmery Katherine Moody was born. Thank you God for answering our prayers. Thank you for your goodness and your mercy!

It is oh, so tempting to grow discouraged when things take a turn for the worse. When there are obstacles, it seems like faith is a million miles away. But no, He (the Author and Perfecter of our faith) is right here. He commends and honors faith that is not easily thwarted by discouraging circumstances. He loves it when we choose to worship Him and trust His goodness and mercy for healing despite things that seem to scream otherwise, including what looks like Jesus' own refusal to help. This was the dilemma of the desperate mother of a demonized daughter.

He commends and honors faith that is not easily thwarted by discouraging circumstances. He loves it when we choose to worship Him and trust His goodness and mercy for healing despite things that seem to scream otherwise, including what looks like Jesus' own refusal to help.

This Canaanite woman was not a Jew and thus she was not "qualified" to receive healing and help from Jesus. But she was one desperate mother. Despite four rejections that would have driven most people away empty handed with their tail between their legs, she refused to be denied. She knew Jesus' mercy. She was convinced of His goodness. She was a woman of great faith!

> And Jesus went away from there and withdrew to the district of Tyre and Sidon. And behold, a Canaanite woman from that region came out and was crying, "Have mercy on me, O Lord, Son of David; my daughter is severely oppressed by a demon." But he did not answer her a word. And his disciples came and begged him, saying, "Send her away, for she is crying out after us." He answered, "I was sent only to the lost sheep of the house of Israel." But she came and knelt before him, saying, "Lord, help me." And he answered, "It is not right to take the children's bread and throw it to the dogs." She said, "Yes, Lord, yet even the dogs eat the crumbs that fall from their masters' table." Then Jesus answered her, "O woman, great is your faith! Be it done for you as you desire." And her daughter was healed instantly. Matthew 15:21-28 ESV

Great faith does not give up—even when others try to interfere and it appears that Jesus says no! Great faith is not diminished by words that relegate you to a "dog" and seem to imply you are unqualified to receive. Great faith is convinced of Jesus' mercy and His goodness. Great faith gets results from Jesus. Jesus truly cares! Although it may not always look like Jesus is compassionate, it is critical that we seek to comprehend the mercy, the goodness and the compassion of Jesus for all who are hurting. Some picture God so far off, so cold, so indifferent and so uncaring. But Jesus shows us exactly who the Father is and what the Father feels for His children. I love how author Ken Blue describes Jesus' compassion:

> The kind of compassion Jesus had for people was not merely an expression of his will, but an eruption from deep within his being. The word used to describe his compassion expresses the involuntary gasp wrenched from a man overwhelmed by a great sorrow or the

> *groan of a woman savaged by labor pains. Out of this deep compassion passion sprang Jesus' mighty works of rescue, healing and deliverance. Ken Blue. Authority to Heal (Kindle Locations 645-648). Kindle Edition.*

Ken continues,

> *In Mark 1:40-41, we find a man who embodies all the physical, social and spiritual disintegration of a sinful world. At this sight, Jesus is overwrought with compassion. A man with leprosy came to him and begged him on his knees, "If you are willing, you can make me clean." Filled with compassion, Jesus reached out his hand and touched the man. "I am willing," he said. "Be clean!" This intensely emotive language describing Jesus (and therefore God) is not peculiar to the Gospel writers. The entire New Testament witnesses to the truth that God's heart is moved for us and his power is near to us in our distress. Ken Blue. Authority to Heal (Kindle Locations 655-659). Kindle Edition.*

God's heart is moved for us and His power is near to us in our distress. Let's choose to trust His mercy and His goodness despite any obstacle that stands in our way. He is a compassionate God who is willing to heal each and every one of us.

Faith in Jesus' Healing Despite Your Faults

"I'm not worthy to have Jesus heal my PTSD," sighed Scott (not his real name), a weary war veteran. "I've made too many mistakes and I know I am not good enough to receive healing. If I could just get a good night's sleep once in awhile, I would be satisfied. Can you pray for that?" Here was a man who had served his country in Afghanistan, suffered through horrific battles and now was tormented with constant night terrors and daily anxiety. And he had no faith at all because he thought he had to be "good enough." He was willing to settle for a few hours of sleep. Being "good enough" is never a requirement for receiving Jesus' healing because Jesus Himself makes each person good enough. That is actually the Good News! When a person believes that Jesus takes all one's sin, making him or her good enough and worthy enough because of Jesus' work on the Cross, then a person is freed to have faith for healing. Faith in Jesus as our Savior, Deliverer, Messiah changes everything and qualifies us for more than a few hours of nightmare-free sleep.

If ever there was a person who would have thought he was not "good enough" to receive Jesus' healing, it was Bartimaeus, a blind beggar who sat by the dusty Jericho road, rejected by society, reduced to panhandling in order to survive. That did not stop him from crying out loudly to Jesus:

> And they came to Jericho. And as he was leaving Jericho with his disciples and a great crowd, Bartimaeus, a blind beggar, the son of Timaeus, was sitting by the roadside. And when he heard that it was Jesus of Nazareth, he began to cry out and say, "Jesus, Son of David, have mercy on me!" And many rebuked him, telling him to be silent. But he cried out all the more, "Son of David, have mercy on me!" And Jesus stopped and said, "Call him." And they called the blind man, saying to him, "Take heart. Get up; he is calling you." And throwing off his cloak, he sprang up and came to Jesus. And Jesus said to him, "What do you want me to do for you?" And the blind man said to him, "Rabbi, let me recover my sight." And Jesus said to him, "Go your way; your faith has made you well." And immediately he recovered his sight and followed him on the way. Mark 10:46-52 ESV

Not only did Bartimaeus have the obstacles of blindness, poverty and social rejection to overcome, he also had many bystanders who were basically telling him to "shut up!" as he cried out when Jesus passed by. Yet Bartimaeus was bold, loud and persistent in calling out to Jesus. He somehow knew those obstacles could not stop Jesus from healing him. He did not look at himself and his "issues" with pity, allowing his circumstances to diminish his desire and his determination. Instead, Bartimaeus looked to Jesus whom he brazenly, yet confidently, addressed as Son of David. This is significant. The title "Son of David" is more than a statement of physical genealogy. It is a Messianic title. When persons referred to Jesus as the Son of David, they meant that they believed He was the long-awaited Deliverer, the fulfillment of the Old Testament prophecies. Yes, when Bartimaeus called Jesus the "Son of David," he expressed his faith that He was the Messiah. Bartimaeus had faith in Jesus, not in himself! And such faith compelled Jesus to ask him to be clear as to what he wanted from Jesus. It seems obvious that a blind man would want to receive his sight, but Jesus loves for us to be specific, be clear: What do YOU want ME to do for you? None of this, "Well, whatever Jesus wants to give me, I'll take. Maybe He will give me a few coins for supper." No! Bartimaeus was clear: "I want to see!" And Jesus wasted no time in commending him, "Go your way; your faith has made you well."

> Jesus wants us well. He is our Deliverer from anything that stands in the way of our healing. We can have faith in Him.

Jesus wants us well. He is our Deliverer from anything that stands in the way of our healing. We can have faith in Him. And that is exactly what Scott, the veteran afflicted with PTSD, experienced as we spoke the truth to him and Jesus set him totally free–free to enjoy whole nights of peaceful sleep and entire days with no anxiety.

But, what if we do believe that Jesus makes us good enough and He alone is our Deliverer and still no healing? There are many different factors that may be involved. Each person's situation is unique. But this I know: Jesus is eager to reveal to you what you need to know, to do, to change and how to cooperate with Him so healing can come.

I experienced this in a powerful way while waiting for healing to come for infertility. We had prayed almost twelve months earlier and still no healing. I was growing very discouraged and was ready to give up hope of ever conceiving our own child. Then we got a call from the local adoption agency. Several years earlier we had put our name on the list for an infant and had gone through all the preliminary steps to receiving a child. The agency was letting us know we were next on the list and would have a baby soon. While this was not what we wanted(although we are supporters of adoption and know that God is, too), we were ready to agree and receive the newborn. However, God nudged our hearts and asked why we were adopting a baby? My honest reply was, "Because I really do not believe that you are going to come through with our healing."

There it was—my own admission of doubt and unbelief. I was not aware how strong this was in my heart until the adoption agency's offer of a baby came. I cried out to Jesus to forgive my unbelief, and as the Author and Perfecter of my faith, to please strengthen faith in my heart. We then notified the agency that the baby should go to the next couple on the list and we trusted Jesus afresh for what we wanted Him to do for us—heal my body and give us a child. Almost nine months to the date, I gave birth to our first child, a healthy eight pound son, Jonathan David Leman. Jesus wants to talk with us, help us, instruct us and correct us so faith can come to our hearts and we can receive what we want Jesus to do for us.

Faith Comes by Hearing...

My understanding of biblical faith has been greatly enhanced by reading an older book, The Real Faith by Dr. Charles Price.

> He has unique and valuable insights in regards to faith for healing and all his writing can be summed up in one statement he makes over and over: "Seek the Healer, not the healing."

While some of the language is awkward, I have learned much from this minister who saw thousands of people healed of cancers, paralysis, mental torment, chronic pain, and so much more. He has unique and valuable insights in regards to faith for healing and all his writing can be summed up in one statement he makes over and over: "Seek the Healer, not the healing." Yes, Jesus is the focus of all that Dr. Price writes. Jesus is the Author of our faith. Jesus wants to release mountain-moving faith in all of our hearts. I love that! In regards to how faith comes to us, Dr. Price writes:

> *Know ye not that faith cometh by hearing, and hearing by the Word of God? In my Greek Testament it reads, "and hearing by a word of God." There is a finer ear than the one with which we listen to the music of the organ in the church service. There is another ear than the one we use when we listen to the reading of the grand old Book.*

It is not merely the intonation of a human voice that speaks as the Bible is read, for men hear that Book and yet do not hear the voice of God. The Bible is a book through which God speaks; yet all do not hear His voice in the lines! Faith cometh by hearing, and hearing by a word of God. Let Jesus speak to this heart of mine and doubts will take the wings of the morning and fly away. Let Jesus breathe a little word to this poor mind of mine and heaven is brought to earth. Fear is gone like a shadow in the light of His glorious truth. Price, Charles S. The Real Faith (pp. 70-71). Jawbone Digital. Kindle Edition.

He continues,

One thing I do know, and that is, I cannot produce faith. Neither in me—nor in you—are there the ingredients or qualities which when mixed, or put together, will make even a mustard seed of Bible faith. If this be true, are we not foolish to attempt to bring about results without it? If I want to cross a lake, and find there is no way to reach the other side, except by boat, would it not be foolish of me to struggle to get across without a boat? The thing I should seek is the boat— not the other side of the lake! Get the boat, and it will take you there. There are certain things which we receive by faith and only by faith. There is not the slightest ambiguity regarding that in the Word. Rather it sets forth a clear declaration of the truth. Now where do we get the faith which will take us across our "lakes"? The answer to this question is positive and sure! Between the covers of the sacred Book there is mention made of faith as the gift of God and faith as a fruit of the Spirit. 'Whether it be gift or fruit, however, the source and origin of faith remains the same! It comes from God. There is no other source of faith; for it is the Faith of God! Suppose you could obtain faith by mixing any spiritual qualities, you might like to mention, in the crucibles of life. Suppose that faith was something you possessed. Now we all know of its power! Would it not be a dangerous possession? Suppose we could use it to cross the lake when God wanted us on this side? Suppose you or I had faith enough this morning to raise up every sufferer among us. If we were to utilize such power, how do we know but what we might be contravening the divine will, and overthrowing the divine plan? Price, Charles S. The Real Faith (pp. 74-75). Jawbone Digital. Kindle Edition.

Dr. Price knows what he is talking about. He has seen blind eyes opened, deaf ears healed and crippled limbs be made whole. He concludes,

> *Let me repeat. He gives us the necessary faith for all things that are in accordance with His blessed will. That faith is first given and then grows as a fruit of the Spirit. But for the mountain-moving faith which banishes disease and sweeps away all barriers by miraculous power, I still maintain that such faith is possible only when it is imparted and that when it is the Savior's will. So, put all your trust in Jesus, for your help cometh alone from Him. Lean hard on the Master's breast, for only as you contact Him can you drink in the sweetness of His presence; and let not the devil deceive you into believing in the power of your own spiritual attainments—for without the Man of Calvary you can do nothing. Trust Him when faith is withheld, and praise Him when it is given. Remember that "He doeth all things well." You and I would blunder and err along the pathway, were it not for His restraining and withholding hand, as well as His bounteous provision for our every need. The things that seem good to you today, could wear the robes of sorrow in your tomorrows. How much better it is to let Him have His way with you, than to always try to have your way with Him. That is my message. It is Jesus! Only Jesus. The Christ of Calvary who is the Giver of every good and perfect gift is also the Author and Finisher of your faith. Rejoice in the love that will not let you go! Be happy in the presence of a Friend who knows you better than you know yourself. Price, Charles S. The Real Faith (pp. 91-92). Jawbone Digital. Kindle Edition.*

There is so much more in this little book that the Holy Spirit has used to strengthen my faith and banish unbelief from my heart.

Jesus is Not Happy with Unbelief

Jesus knows how detrimental unbelief is and He often seems surprised that we struggle to overcome unbelief. In His own hometown, Jesus could heal only a few people because of the unbelief.

> He went away from there and came to his hometown, and his disciples followed him. And on the Sabbath he began to teach in the synagogue, and many who heard him were astonished, saying, "Where did this man get these things? What is the wisdom given to him? How are such mighty works done by his hands? Is not this the carpenter, the son of Mary and brother of James and Joses and Judas and Simon? And are not his sisters here with us?" And they took offense at him. And Jesus said to them, "A prophet is not without honor, except in his hometown and among his relatives and in his own household." And he could do no mighty work there, except that he laid his hands on a few sick people and healed them. And he marveled because of their unbelief. Mark 6:1-6 ESV

What didn't they believe? Healing? Miracles? No, they believed in works of wonder. But, they did not believe in the Person of Jesus. They saw Him as an ordinary carpenter's son and their hearts were clouded with dishonor. Jesus was downright shocked at their unbelief. Any distorted picture we might have of Jesus can hinder our faith. The Holy Spirit is so helpful in revealing the truth and the One who is the Truth.

> Jesus was downright shocked at their unbelief. Any distorted picture we might have of Jesus can hinder our faith. The Holy Spirit is so helpful in revealing the truth and the One who is the Truth.

On another occasion Jesus had some pretty strong words to say about unbelief. He descended from the Mount of Transfiguration to find a large crowd in a tizzy because His disciples had failed to deliver a boy from a serious demonic oppression. Jesus was not happy! And He specifically addressed their unbelief.

And when they came to the disciples, they saw a great crowd around them, and scribes arguing with them. And immediately all the crowd, when they saw him, were greatly amazed and ran up to him and greeted him. And he asked them, "What are you arguing about with them?" And someone from the crowd answered him, "Teacher, I brought my son to you, for he has a spirit that makes him mute. And whenever it seizes him, it throws him down, and he foams and grinds his teeth and becomes rigid. So I asked your disciples to cast it out, and they were not able." And he answered them, "O faithless generation, how long am I to be with you? How long am I to bear with you? Bring him to me." And they brought the boy to him. And when the spirit saw him, immediately it convulsed the boy, and he fell on the ground and rolled about, foaming at the mouth. And Jesus asked his father, "How long has this been happening to him?" And he said, "From childhood. And it has often cast him into fire and into water, to destroy him. But if you can do anything, have compassion on us and help us." And Jesus said to him, "'If you can'! All things are possible for one who believes." Immediately the father of the child cried out and said, "I believe; help my unbelief!" And when Jesus saw that a crowd came running together, he rebuked the unclean spirit, saying to it, "You mute and deaf spirit, I command you, come out of him and never enter him again." And after crying out and convulsing him terribly, it came out, and the boy was like a corpse, so that most of them said, "He is dead." But Jesus took him by the hand and lifted him up, and he arose. Mark 9:14-27 ESV

This same incident is also recorded by Matthew and we looked at this earlier, but Matthew gives us more insight about unbelief and what Jesus says to do about it.

Then the disciples came to Jesus privately and said, "Why could we not cast it out?"So Jesus said to them, "Because of your unbelief;for assuredly, I say to you, if you have faith as a mustard seed, you will say to this mountain, 'Move from here to there,' and

it will move; and nothing will be impossible for you. However, this kind does not go out except by prayer and fasting." Matthew 17:19-21 NKJV

Jesus is clear that all things are possible to the person who believes and He seems to indicate that this is not difficult. I do not pretend to understand this, let alone live this. Jesus did tell us this kind only goes out by prayer and fasting. Again, we do not engage in prayer and fasting to "get something from God." No, we spend time in prayer, talking with Him, listening to Him, allowing Him to expose our unbelief and hindrances to the faith He wants to impart so mountains can be removed and people healed. This is Jesus' desire for us! We do not have to beg Him to impart faith to our hearts. He is ready to equip us to so His will.

That You May Believe...

What are some next steps so we may be strengthened in our faith? John, Jesus' closest friend, spends more time in his Gospel talking about "believe" than any other writer of the New Testament. He knows something about faith. He summarizes with this statement:

And truly Jesus did many other signs in the presence of His disciples, which are not written in this book; but these are written that you may believe that Jesus is the Christ, the Son of God, and that believing you may have life in His name. John 20:30-31 NKJV

Are you struggling to believe? Start reading or re-reading the Gospels and invite the Holy Spirit to release fresh faith in your heart. These are written that we may believe and believing, have life in Jesus' name.

Discussion Questions

1. When was a time you lived through a crisis in faith? When was a time you didn't?

2. Read Mark 5:25-34. What are some things that you notice about the woman who had suffered with constant bleeding? How do these observations apply in your life today?

3. Why is it important to continue to seek God and exercise your faith, even when you don't feel like it?

Chapter **4**

Jesus Heals
Miraculously

A Supernatural God

Before the Lord called me into ministry, I was on track for a career in science, physics to be precise.

My father has worked for a denominational office in communications since before I was born. As a result, faith and the church have always been a central part of my life. When I took physics in high school, it was like everything clicked. I was made to do this.

I know physics is an abstract and difficult subject for most. It is a subject reserved for oddballs and geniuses. Before you think too much of me, I should let you know that I'm not sure I could do anything other than physics like I could do physics. I routinely struggled with subjects like literature and history. Even mathematics didn't make a lot of sense until I took physics and then understood how mathematics could be applied to something "useful."

After taking physics in high school I knew I had to continue down that road. I majored in physics in college, and while finishing my undergraduate degree I realized I hadn't learned everything I wanted to. I decided to apply to graduate school. I was accepted and eventually earned a Ph.D. in theoretical quantum mechanics at University of Illinois. It was after that when God transitioned me to ministry.

One question I routinely get asked is how I made the transition from the realm of science into believing and practicing a supernatural healing ministry. It's not often you find someone who has walked both of those paths.

The truth is, I'm not convinced that science and faith, even supernatural faith, are at odds. There are many people who believe they are, but those who are experts in the field are less closed-minded about such matters than you might think. My experience in science was never at odds with my faith. Rather, I saw science as an exploration of God's design. God could have made this world any one of a million different ways—the way He chose to do so tells us something about Him.

God created all that exists, the natural realm and the supernatural realm. He created the world that is best described by science and the world described to us by Scripture. If you want to study God's natural created order, dive into the sciences. See God's cosmic fingerprint in the way He wove together our world. Don't make the mistake, however, of thinking that natural structure describes all that there is.

> Christianity is fundamentally a supernatural faith. One cannot remove the supernatural and retain the essence of Christianity.

Christianity is fundamentally a supernatural faith. One cannot remove the supernatural and retain the essence of Christianity. Sure, you might glean Christian teachings about morality or wisdom, but the kernel from which Christianity grows has been lost. We believe in a God who spoke this world into being and breathed His life into our ancestors' lungs. We believe in a God who chose and directed a man named Abraham to move across the world to start a new story of faith. We believe in a God who supernaturally decimated the world's greatest power at the time with ten crippling plagues and delivered His chosen nation by walking them right out of the country through the ocean. We believe in a God who answered Elijah's prayers with fire and carried him off to heaven in a whirlwind.

When that God takes up residence in a man named Jesus, the story is no less supernatural. This Jesus is the offspring of a virgin, announced by angels and prophets. After He grows up, He turns water into wine and walks across the sea. He heals the sick, delivers the demonized and even resurrects the dead. Our God is a supernatural God and His realm is the realm of miracles.

Natural and Supernatural Healing

As we saw earlier, it is God's will for us to be whole and well. Healing is God's desire for us. In fact, God works healing through both the natural and supernatural realms. God has designed our bodies to have incredible healing capacities.

When I was young, I broke my left forearm. While playing a game with my dad and brother, I tripped and fell into a cast-iron staircase railing. The impact broke both bones in my forearm, which criss-crossed in an "X" pattern. After informing my parents of my broken arm (which was now hanging with a bend in the middle of it), we made a rapid trip to the hospital where the doctors set my arm and a cast on it.

I spent all summer in that cast–a major disappointment for a young boy. However, coming out the far end of that experience, my arm was healed. If you think about it, it really is quite incredible. My bones grew back together. They were broken clean through and they grew back together. Just by putting them in the right place and keeping them still enough, my body knew what to do to repair that drastic break. It really is incredible.

The body, of course, has many other self-healing capabilities. Whether it is our immune system able to develop our own resistance to germs or the way our skin and blood vessels restore themselves after a cut, our body can repair and restore itself from a variety of injuries and assaults.

There is a limit to how far our body's self-healing capacities can take us though. We do not have the capacity to naturally recover from every ailment. Sometimes an infection or disease takes over beyond our body's ability to fight it off, as happens in cancer or with HIV. Some damage our body does not have the ability to recover from, such as a severed spinal cord or detached retina. Sometimes, for example in diabetes, the body's ingrained processes break down beyond the body's ability to self-repair.

Medical science continues to advance and help provide new solutions. A detached retina, for example can often be repaired surgically. Diabetes can be managed with insulin shots. Praise God for these advances; God not only provides the supernatural power that results in the miraculous, but also the gifts of intelligence and insight that help mankind partner with the body to bring healing. Both are methods of healing and while I will always champion for God's in-breaking miraculous power, there is no need to throw out the medical community either. God will use medical science to bring us healing, just as He will use the power of the Spirit to bring us healing. And when there is no road forward according to medical science, God's supernatural power has the capacity to address any condition:

> And Jesus went throughout all the cities and villages, teaching in their synagogues and proclaiming the gospel of the kingdom and healing every disease and every affliction. Matthew 9:35 ESV

Did you catch that? Healing every disease and every affliction. Medical science may or may not have anything to offer your situation. Whether it does or not, God's supernatural healing does.

Our Supernatural God

If we're honest with ourselves, many of us fully embrace the natural methods of healing and hold a lot more skepticism toward God's supernatural intervention, particularly if whatever ails us can be treated medically. It's not uncommon for me to pray with people and not expect God to heal them because it could be addressed medically.

I find the thinking behind this somewhat bizarre. God isn't in heaven with a limited supply of miracles. He isn't rationing them out to those who are most qualified. It doesn't tire Him out to provide His supernatural power so He doesn't bother if there is another solution. No, God likes to work the miraculous. We don't inconvenience Him when we ask for His power to bring healing. Healing is a part of His character. In the Old Testament, God even reveals one of the names He is known by as "The Lord our Healer" (Exodus 15:26). God calls Himself by that name because healing is a passion of His and part of His nature.

Did Jesus heal because He had compassion on the needs of the people He encountered? Absolutely. Scripture is clear about that. But that notwithstanding, He also healed because He wanted to. He likes to heal people. I mean, if you were God, wouldn't you find it fun to release your supernatural power and bring healing?

> Did Jesus heal because He had compassion on the needs of the people He encountered? Absolutely. Scripture is clear about that. But that notwithstanding, He also healed because He wanted to. He likes to heal people.

In John 5, we see that part of the reason the Jews sought to kill Jesus was because He healed people on the Sabbath. That was just too far outside their grid and it rendered Jesus a law-breaker (as if healing was something accomplished by our own efforts). In Luke, Jesus heals a woman on the Sabbath who had been bent over for eighteen years. As usual, it provokes some discussion:

> But the ruler of the synagogue, indignant because Jesus has healed on the Sabbath, said to the people, "There are six days in which work ought to be done. Come on those days and be healed, not on the Sabbath day. Luke 13:14 ESV

The synagogue ruler is essentially saying, "Look, come back tomorrow. Can't you just hold off one day and do healing tomorrow?" It doesn't seem too much to ask, and for Jesus it seems like a strategically wise choice. Why bother healing people on the one day that is going to turn the religious leaders against you; why not wait one more day?

> *Then the Lord answered him, "You hypocrites! Does not each of you on the Sabbath untie his ox or his donkey from the manger and lead it away to water it? And ought not this woman, a daughter of Abraham whom Satan has bound for eighteen years be loosed from this bond on the Sabbath day?"* Luke 13:15-16 ESV

Jesus' reply essentially boils down to this: I don't want to wait, and I don't think it's right. I don't think it's right to wait one more day, even if that is controversial and inconvenient. Even if it contributes to getting me killed, I want to heal her right now.

God is not inconvenienced by us seeking His supernatural healing. He likes to heal and He wants to do it. Even if you don't "need" His power because there is another solution, Jesus likes to heal because He enjoys healing people. God loves to bring His supernatural power into our conditions and afflictions.

The Miraculous Today

Jesus continued to work miracles through His body of believers after He ascended back to heaven. Paul, writing about the gifts of the Spirit poured out on the church specifically lists both healing and miracles:

> *...to another gifts of healing by the one Spirit, to another the working of miracles...* 1 Corinthians 12:9-10 ESV

Paul's logic in this passage is that because we all share of the same Spirit, when the Spirit begins to manifest (1 Corinthians 12:7), we should be looking for these gifts to be poured out on the body. We all have access to these same gifts. Jesus still heals through His supernatural power on the earth; but now that power of the Spirit flows through the church, you and me.

Learning to work miracles is about learning to see what the Spirit is doing and partnering with Him (John 5:19). The working of miracles is described as a manifestation of the Spirit, a way the invisible Spirit makes Himself concrete. We carry in ourselves the authority to release the kingdom of God, but the power for the miraculous is released in cooperation with the Spirit. As we grow in our ability to recognize the Spirit at work and partner with Him, we can see the miraculous happen.

In Genesis 1, we see the account of God creating the world. There may be no passage of Scripture where so much of His power is so clearly evident as in the creation of all things. As such, it's a wonderful place to look to understand the dynamics of how God's power is released in creation.

In the creation account, God first creates the universe, but the world was "without form and void" (Genesis 1:2). There was messiness, chaos, disorder. It wasn't what God had in His mind to create. How did God create the world we live in from this primordial mess?

There were two elements. First, "And the Spirit of God was hovering over the face of the waters," (Genesis 1:2). The Spirit was hovering over the chaos and brokenness. Second, "And God said, 'Let there be light,' and there was light," (Genesis 1:3). Into the hovering presence of the Spirit, God speaks His Word. When the Word of God meets the hovering presence of the Spirit of God, a new reality is catalyzed and created. The two of these coming together creates order out of chaos —life where there is no life.

This is indeed the same dynamic we partner with today. As we learn to discern the hovering presence over the chaos in someone's life, the brokenness in their body, the division in their relationships, the pain in their emotions, we get to add the words. God now deals in our hearts through faith and we get to speak the words into the hovering presence of the Spirit and see new realities catalyzed.

I would encourage you to consider examining some the miraculous accounts in the Scripture and look for this dynamic. Here is a particularly clear account where God's power is released through the Word meeting the hovering presence of the Spirit:

> Now at Lystra there was a man sitting who could not use his feet. He was crippled from birth and had never walked. He listened to Paul speaking. And Paul, looking intently at him and **seeing that he had the faith to be made well, said in a loud voice,** "Stand upright on your feet." And he sprang up and began walking. Acts 14:8-10 ESV

Paul looks out on the crowd and sees the hovering presence of a gift of faith (also in 1 Corinthians 12). When he sees the Spirit hovering over the man and releasing this faith, he adds his words and works a dramatic miracle.

Having Eyes to See

A question that immediately comes to mind is this: how do we do that? What does it look like to see the Spirit hovering over the chaos or disorder in someone's life?

These are important questions and answering them involves taking a lifelong journey. Learning how to see the hovering presence of the Spirit is something God wants to teach us as we walk this journey of learning to partner with Him.

The founder of the Vineyard church movement (Dianne and I both work at a Vineyard church) used a catchy phrase to discuss the process of learning to see what God is doing: "Some things are better caught than taught." By this he meant that it is the life-on-life experience of learning to minister along with other people that helps reproduce these skills. I could describe different ways you might learn to see the Spirit touching people, but that is no comparison for being in the trenches together.

This really is the reason we started the School of Kingdom Ministry. We felt it was important to create a reproducible, experiential environment where people could "catch" these kinds of skills and abilities. Over the last few years we've seen thousands of our students around the world effectively trained and released in the things of the Spirit. If this book is whetting your appetite to live out this ministry, you might see if School of Kingdom Ministry would be a good fit at your church. At the risk of sounding a bit sales-pitchy, there just isn't a more effective mechanism local churches can use to step into the things of the Spirit as a community.

A Modern Miracle

I'd like to conclude with a modern story. A few years ago I was down in Brazil with Happy Leman (Dianne's husband) and one other pastor from our church. We were there as part of a ministry training trip that Randy Clark was leading, practicing being in environments where things could be "caught."

The final service of the week-long trip was a healing service. We were at a new church Randy had not partnered with before and the plan for the service was to have Randy teach on healing, followed by the ministry team giving words of knowledge for healing and concluding with a time of prayer.

When the time came to give words of knowledge*, I had a distinct impression that someone had a problem with the vertebrae about midway down the back. I turned around and pointed to a spot just below my shoulder blades on my spine. The rest of the team gave their words of knowledge and we waited for people to respond and get prayer.

Low and behold, the first person to come my way was a gentleman in a wheelchair! Not only that, but he has a steel brace that went around his midsection keeping his chest and back immobilized. Yikes, I thought! This is a doozy! One other ministry team member came up and we began to ask questions about his condition to figure out how to pray.

The man told us that about six years earlier he had fallen off a third-story roof and broken his back. His spinal cord wasn't severed, but it was so severely damaged that his doctor warned him if he ever tried to walk again, his back could break and he would be paralyzed. He was confined to his wheelchair permanently, and in constant pain.

I was honestly disappointed because I knew there was no way I could pray for this man and ask him to get up and walk. But sometimes commanding the impossible releases the miracle needed. We started to pray. My teammate and I began to command the back to be made whole and to be restored.

After just a couple of minutes, the man got our attention and told us he wanted to get up and try to walk. I didn't want to ask that of him, but if he had faith and felt a leading to do that, I was willing to partner with him. The two of us helped him up and balanced him as he began to try and walk. His leg muscles had atrophied for six years and his balance was very poor, but he began to put one foot in front of the other, and with each passing yard he was walking with more strength and stability.

After about fifteen or twenty feet, he remarked to us that he didn't need his back brace anymore. He reached down and unstrapped it. I

---

*A Word of Knowledge is another one of the gifts Paul lists in 1 Corinthians 12 and essentially a fact or bit of information the Spirit communicates to you. In this case, we were asking God for leadings about what conditions people in the meeting had that He was releasing power to heal.

was shocked! He removed it and began walking freely across the front of the church, continuing to grow in strength, confidence and balance with each step.

His friends were there, flabberghasted. They said in the last six years they had never seen him walk like this. He always went straight from bed to the wheelchair and back to bed at the end of the day. Shock and joy were written on their faces.

The gentleman walked across the space in front of the stage and took a seat on the far side. I walked over to him and asked how he felt. He said he felt good, stronger than he was used to. At the end of the night, he put his old back brace into his wheelchair and wheeled his own wheelchair out the back of the church.

I certainly don't experience miracles that dramatic every time I pray, but I am seeing them a lot more often. More importantly, I don't know that I really had all that much to do with that miracle. I simply prayed some simple, direct prayers for a few minutes. He was the one who acted in faith, and Jesus was the one who released power.

> If He did it for me, why not you? Why wouldn't Jesus want to pull you up and give you a front row seat while He releases His miraculous power?

When we come to the subject of the miraculous, it can be easy to think we're missing something and can't be used that powerfully. Maybe we don't think we're holy enough or close enough to God. All I know is that the miracle Jesus worked there wasn't because of anything I had. It honestly felt like I just got to be up front and center and I was fortunate enough to watch Jesus work the miraculous. If He did it for me, why not you? Why wouldn't Jesus want to pull you up and give you a front row seat while He releases His miraculous power? It could happen the next time you step out in obedience and pray.

Discussion Questions

1. Have you been open or closed to the idea of supernatural healing? Why?

2. Have you ever witnessed a miracle, healing or otherwise? If so, share the story.

3. If you could experience one miracle in your life today, what would it be?

Chapter 5

Jesus Wants Us Whole

Forgive in Order to Conceive?

A small team of us sat with Naomi (not her real name) and listened to her heartbreaking journey to conceive a second child. Several miscarriages, including one the previous month, had robbed her of all hope. She despaired that she would ever carry another child to full term. There would never be the much wanted sibling for her six-year-old son. As always, we asked the Holy Spirit to direct our prayer for healing and encouraged Naomi to be alert for any thoughts or pictures that popped into her mind.

After a minute or two, we saw tears welling up in her eyes, so we paused to ask what she was thinking. She then relayed a very painful image of her father, an African polygamist tribal chief who had emotionally and physically abused her during her adolescent years. She was now living far away in the United States and had little contact with him. However, the ugly anger that rose in her heart frightened her, and as she told her tragic story, she began to tremble uncontrollably and heave great sobs of sorrow.

Our team knew what was needed. We spoke the comfort and healing of the Holy Spirit to her and waited until she was still. Then, we gently explained the power of unforgiveness to block healing from flowing to one's body. After giving her some simple instructions, we led her in forgiving her father for his unspeakable crimes against her. This is only possible with the help of the Holy Spirit, but it is powerful and freeing. We followed this with a few simple healing prayers for her womb and blessed her to conceive soon. Peace flooded her whole being. I was not surprised but, of course overjoyed, when she ran up to me a month later at church and radiantly proclaimed, "I'm pregnant!" When she was freed from unforgiveness in her heart and her emotions, her body was freed to conceive and carry another child. I have witnessed similar healings of infertility hundreds of times in the last thirty years. These testify to me that physical healing must often be approached from a view of the whole person—body, mind and spirit.

Wait, do you mean if I don't forgive everyone that has harmed me or if I don't deal with hidden sins or issues, Jesus refuses to heal me? Do I have to forgive in order to conceive or be healed of my condition? Do I have to clean myself up so Jesus will touch me and make me whole? No! Jesus does not require us to "meet the conditions" and then He will dole out healing. It can sound that way and that is sometimes how people present it, but it is not at all what Jesus wants nor means. He is the forgiver. He has paid the price for all to be made whole—in our entire being—body, mind and spirit. And He loves us, every bit of us!

Jesus Cares About Our Entire Being

Jesus cares about our entire being because Jesus wants us whole. He knows how interrelated He created each of us, and He wants us to be made entirely whole, not just a "part" of us.

Jesus cares about our entire being because Jesus wants us whole. He knows how interrelated He created each of us, and He wants us to be made entirely whole, not just a "part" of us. That is why Jesus came to take all of our sins, all of our sicknesses, all of our oppression and to heal our broken hearts, too. Jesus' bold proclamation made clear His intentions:

> "The Spirit of the Lord is upon me, because he has anointed me to proclaim good news to the poor. He has sent me to proclaim liberty to the captives and recovering of sight to the blind, to set at liberty those who are oppressed, to proclaim the year of the Lord's favor." Luke 4:18-19 ESV

When it comes to healing, Jesus cares about every aspect of our lives—physical, mental, emotional, relational, spiritual and even financial. His desire is that we are made completely whole, with no "broken" or damaged parts. Jesus is our Savior and He wants us saved—completely. That word saved is the Greek word sozo which denotes being healthy and whole in our entire being—body, mind, spirit, now and forever. This is so important because many relegate being saved to just "going to heaven someday." Jesus says, "Your faith has saved you," in regards to all types of healing—from sin, sickness, demons. Jesus wants us saved, made whole, healed in every way. This is an essential truth when we seek healing today because it affects how we approach praying for or ministering healing to others. We need to consider the whole person, not a part.

Human beings are not designed to be divided up into different parts. Yes, we all have bodies, minds, and hearts (spirits), but each part should not be treated separately from the others when it comes to healing. This is a common mistake that both medical and spiritual practitioners make. For example, a medical person may treat a headache strictly as a bodily ailment and prescribe pain-killing drugs, but disregard the person's emotional toll that might be the real cause of the headache. As soon as the drug wears off, the pain is still present because the stress has not been addressed. On the other hand, some who pray for healing overemphasize the need for repentance from sin or the need for deliverance from demons. However, these both should be viewed as part of the whole and not as isolated elements in healing. Again, we are a whole being and must be treated as a whole being because our "parts" affect one another. This is wisdom recorded thousands of years ago by Solomon:

A joyful heart is good medicine, but a crushed spirit dries up the bones. Proverbs 17:22 ESV

The Holy Spirit shows us how to minister to each person so each can be made whole. There is real danger in "dissecting the human being" or focusing too much on one aspect and neglecting others.

A joyful or despondent emotional and spiritual disposition do make a difference in our physical body, our actual bones. Jesus wants us whole and free—free from sin, sickness, unforgiveness, demons, poverty and fear. He came to set the captives free and He knows best how to bring wholeness to each individual. Sometimes Jesus addresses our fear first or He casts out a demon or He reminds us to forgive another or He touches our hurting body. Each of these is important, but none should be the only focus in our prayers for healing that lead to wholeness. The Holy Spirit shows us how to minister to each person so each can be made whole. There is real danger in "dissecting the human being" or focusing too much on one aspect and neglecting others. This can even hinder the healing process.

Dangers of Dissecting the Dead

I looked at the catalog of seven pages I was asked to fill out before receiving healing prayer and I plummeted into despair. Question after question stared at me—questions that probed into my past, my ancestors, my parents, my fears and my pains. This history was designed to give the prayer team a starting place for ministry to me. Such an inventory can be helpful, I suppose. The original intent of these questions was to address the "whole person" and not just deal with a part. So far so good. However, this entire approach ended up doing more dissection, not integration of my whole being, and the result was unintentional separation, damage and marginal healing.

I have found, after many years of trying this approach for myself and others, it really does not work. Such healing paradigms are misguided ways to bring the wholeness Jesus wants for us. The basic problem is often these approaches to healing are not grounded in a biblical view of wholeness and concentrate too much on fixing the "old me" or regurgitating my sinful past. But the "old me" has been made clean and new by faith in Jesus. Therefore, I liken some of these methods to "putting makeup on a corpse." The techniques are focused on too much interaction with a "dead person," the old me. There is danger in dissecting the dead or in attempting an extreme makeover on one. What do I mean? When we are born again (John 3: 3-5), we died in Christ, were buried with Him and rose again as a new person. If we want to walk in the wholeness that Jesus has provided for us, we must start with this most foundational truth of the Gospel. As Paul wrote:

> I have been crucified with Christ; and it is no longer I who live, but Christ lives in me; and the life which I now live in the flesh I live by faith in the Son of God, who loved me and gave Himself up for me. Galatians 2:20 NASB

Often our minds need a major renewal concerning the truth of who we are now as a brand new person, filled with the Spirit, empowered to walk free from sin, demons, fear, unforgiveness and sickness, too. There are obstacles to be removed, but we want the Spirit to reveal these.

We are now a new creation and the old has passed away. If we do not start here, we can end up trying to fix the old, dead person instead of removing obstacles for a person to walk in the reality of being a new, righteous, holy and beloved child of God. I am well-aware that we are not automatically transformed into wholeness when we are born again, although that is how our heavenly Father sees us. Our problem is we do not see ourselves as He sees us. Often our minds need a major renewal concerning the truth of who we are now as a brand new person, filled with the Spirit, empowered to walk free from sin, demons, fear, unforgiveness and sickness, too. There are obstacles to be removed, but we want the Spirit to reveal these. We do not want to depend on the exhaustive introspection of our past—a past that

Jesus says is now dead, buried and gone. He is the Spirit of truth and is faithful to expose anything that keeps us in bondage.

As we learn the truth and pay attention to what God's Word says, we receive life and health to our entire being. When we tune into our beliefs and experiences that possibly hinder our wholeness, we can surrender these to Jesus and trust His healing.

> *My son, give attention to my words; Incline your ear to my sayings. Do not let them depart from your eyes; Keep them in the midst of your heart; For they are **life to those who find them and health to all their flesh**. Keep your heart with all diligence, for out of it spring the issues of life.* Proverbs 4:20-23 NKJV

Jesus wants us whole. Jesus shows each one the truth. This empowers one to abandon lies so healing can come. When we minister healing with this as our foundation, we have seen true wholeness come to people. Jesus wants us free.

Jesus Wants Us Free From Sin

At the center of many physical problems is the issue of sin because sin and sickness are both a result of man's fall and are part of the kingdom of darkness. Through faith in Jesus we are delivered out of that kingdom of darkness and into the kingdom of light where we now experience the forgiveness and freedom from past, present and future sins. This is glorious and good.

> *...May you be filled with joy always thanking the Father. He has enabled you to share in the inheritance that belongs to his people, who live in the light. For he has rescued us from the kingdom of darkness and transferred us into the Kingdom of his dear Son, who purchased our freedom and forgave our sins.* Colossians 11b-14 NLT

It is quite common for people to argue about the truth that Jesus frees us from ALL sin—past, present and future. However, this is one of the most critical truths for wholeness. Jesus Himself foreshadowed this several times even before He was crucified, and He showed the important connection between sickness, sin and our wholeness. Here is one account:

> Now there is in Jerusalem by the Sheep Gate a pool, in Aramaic called Bethesda, which has five roofed colonnades. In these lay a multitude of invalids—blind, lame, and paralyzed. One man was there who had been an invalid for thirty-eight years. When Jesus saw him lying there and knew that he had already been there a long time, he said to him, "Do you want to be healed?" The sick man answered him, "Sir, I have no one to put me into the pool when the water is stirred up, and while I am going another steps down before me." Jesus said to him, "Get up, take up your bed, and walk." And at once the man was healed, and he took up his bed and walked. ... Afterward Jesus found him in the temple and said to him, "See, you are well! **Sin no more**, that nothing worse may happen to you." John 5:2-14 ESV

"Sin no more" is not something we can accomplish with our own willpower nor is it some sort of "sinless perfection" we strive for. Jesus empowers us to live as a new creation, overcoming sin and its deadly consequences.

Is Jesus saying this man's sin caused his sickness of thirty-eight long years? No! He is revealing that this man can now live as a totally free and whole being, no longer sick or sinning. This is the exact gift Jesus made possible for all when He rose from the dead. Jesus wants us whole and this includes being free from sin and sickness. "Sin no more" is not something we can accomplish with our own willpower nor is it some sort of "sinless perfection" we strive for. Jesus empowers us to live as a new creation, overcoming sin and its deadly consequences. Those consequences are sometimes outright sickness or disease and other times, a tragically messed-up life. Whether our sin gives birth to our sickness or whether our sickness results in sin, or maybe neither of these two (see John 9), there is an interrelationship that Jesus often addresses in order for us to be free. Several years ago, a young man who is part of our church family shared this story with us:

> *This morning at the hotel I went to get a towel and I saw a girl on the phone crying her eyes out! So I asked the dumb question if she was alright and she said, "No (of course, she was crying), I got robbed last night and I'm all alone and have no way of getting home, I have no money and no clue where I'm even at!" At that time the hotel manager came over and took me aside and told me that she was a prostitute. So I went back to her and told her who I was, that I was a Christian and I told her I was going to help her get home. But first I explained to her that it was no mistake I walked out (because there were plenty of people in the breakfast area that walked by her and didn't see her). I told her I thought God wanted me to tell her that he sees her. I told her that everything she had done God doesn't care and that He just to be in her life and that God is going to take care of her from now on and she will never be alone or abandoned again because Jesus is never going to leave her. So I asked if she knew Jesus and she said she had heard of him but didn't know anything about him. I asked her if she wanted to know him and she said yes. I asked if I could pray and she said yes and she gave her life to Jesus and received the Holy Spirit! I talked to her about her experience and she said she feels peace. I then gave her bus money so she could return home.*

This woman was sick in her emotions, her finances, possibly her body, and definitely her spirit. Thankfully, Jesus wanted her whole and she is on that path now. Thanks, too, to a young man who knew it was not enough to just minister to "one part" of a precious human being, but instead brought healing to her whole life. This is the heart of Jesus.

On another occasion, Jesus showed the interrelationship of sin and sickness and how He is the healer of all.

> *And behold, some people brought to him a paralytic, lying on a bed. And when Jesus saw their faith, he said to the paralytic, "Take heart, my son; your sins are forgiven." And behold, some of the scribes*

said to themselves, "This man is blaspheming." But Jesus, knowing their thoughts, said, "Why do you think evil in your hearts? For which is easier, to say, 'Your sins are forgiven,' or to say, 'Rise and walk'? But that you may know that the Son of Man has authority on earth to forgive sins"—he then said to the paralytic—"Rise, pick up your bed and go home." Matthew 9:2-6 ESV

Jesus wants us to be free from sin and to be free from sickness. He has the authority to forgive all sins and He did this with His shed blood, removing any obstacle that sin puts in the way of our physical healing. When we are seeking to be made whole, we are wise to ask, "Lord, is there any area of my life where I am not living in the truth of being set free from sin? Could this in any way be related to my being physically sick?" Time and again we have seen the Holy Spirit so gently, powerfully reveal the truth so people can repent, receive Jesus' forgiveness and be set free. We equip people in our School of Kingdom Ministry to lovingly minister the truth of Jesus' complete forgiveness to people who struggle with sin and are consumed with shame and condemnation. Jesus wants us whole. Jesus wants us free.

> When we are seeking to be made whole, we are wise to ask, "Lord, is there any area of my life where I am not living in the truth of being set free from sin? Could this in any way be related to my being physically sick?"

Jesus Wants Us Free from Demons

Demons are real. Demons have power. But Jesus has all authority over demons and He has given that authority to us so we can be made whole and minister that freedom to others. Jesus wants us free from demons. One of the most prevalent manifestations of demonic oppression today is debilitating depression. Depression is widespread in our culture and afflicts all ages, seriously sabotaging our wholeness. Of course, not all depression is related to a demonic presence, but demons can be a factor that do contribute to depression and its destructive power. Listen to the story of my good friend, Diane, who is an outstanding nurse practitioner in our community and had her own battle with depression.

I was saved on July 2, 1986. In the midst of a painful divorce, I left my mainstream church to attend a faith-based charismatic church. During a time of ministry I asked for healing from depressive symptoms that I was experiencing. One of the women praying for me asked if I was taking an antidepressant, which at the time I was. She told me I needed to get off of it or I would not be able to hear from the Holy Spirit. Being new in the Lord, I complied. Month by month the depression lingered until God sent a former patient of mine to tell me that my mood needed a change and convinced me to go back on medication. In two weeks my symptoms lessened greatly and I returned to a normal life. In the early 90's however, something changed dramatically. I was filled with feelings of loss, worthlessness, self-loathing and hopelessness. I was oppressed to the point that everything I did was forced, I was totally void of energy and though I cried out to God for healing, it didn't come until some ten months later. Kneeling at my bedside, crying uncontrollably I told Jesus that if He didn't heal me I wanted to die. In an instant I both felt and saw the strength and weight of massive claws that surrounded my shoulders. I then felt a greater strength pulling the weight off of my body. At that moment, Jesus delivered me from the oppression of the enemy. Because I experienced something as powerful as this, it took me awhile to really let what happened to me sink in. I began to ask Jesus questions about my experience. The one that sticks in my mind the most was why he allowed me to suffer all of that time? I fully understood his answer when he told me he wanted me to be balanced. I have experienced both depression as well as demonic oppression and in both cases I can say without hesitation that Jesus is the ultimate healer and deliverer no matter what we face. I hope that my story will help many who are oppressed by the devil!

Jesus shows each person how to have freedom. The healing journey may take several turns and take some time, but we can know that Jesus wants us free from demons, Jesus wants us whole. Demons can affect us mentally, physically, and relationally, just like this woman in Jesus' day:

> Now he was teaching in one of the synagogues on the Sabbath. And behold, there was a woman who had had a disabling spirit for eighteen years. She was bent over and could not fully straighten herself. When Jesus saw her, he called her over and said to her, "Woman, you are freed from your disability." And he laid his hands on her, and immediately she was made straight, and she glorified God. ... And ought not this woman, a daughter of Abraham whom Satan bound for eighteen years, be loosed from this bond on the Sabbath day?" Luke 13:10-12, 16 ESV

Jesus addressed this woman as a "daughter of Abraham," a shocking revelation to any religious observer. In the synagogue and Jewish culture overall, women were second-class citizens (especially crippled ones!) and they were definitely NOT considered daughters of father Abraham. Jesus established a very crucial aspect of this woman's wholeness when He affirmed her identity as a daughter—on the Sabbath, in the synagogue—and set her free from the demon who had oppressed her physically for eighteen years. She was loved by God as a daughter. She could now stand tall and strong. She was truly free.

In our School of Kingdom Ministry we equip believers to free others who are oppressed by demons. We give you a brief outline of this in our list of resources in the appendix. This is a critical piece in the puzzle of our wholeness.

Jesus Wants Us Free to Forgive

My good friends, Bill and Connie, had enjoyed thirty-two years of married life until everything suddenly came crashing down when Bill confessed to serious infidelity. It would take a few miracles from the Holy Spirit to bring restoration to their broken relationship and broken hearts, but at the core of their healing was the power of Jesus' forgiveness—received and given.

Connie writes: On January 12, 2012, Bill revealed to me that our marriage of 32 years was not what I thought it was. Bill confessed that he had had multiple affairs for the past ten years of our marriage, had a plan to leave me and already had an apartment. Needless to say, I was devastated, broken and blindsided. I had no idea. Bill left me that night. The next day, we had several conversations, but there were two pivotal ones that were the turning points in Bill's life and our marriage. I told Bill I was so worried about him and didn't know he was so lost. Bill was a sergeant in the Illinois State Police, and I was afraid he would get in his squad car and possibly be killed, and would go to hell. I told him he needed to get back with God. Bill expressed to me that I could never forgive him for all that he had done. He had done too much damage to our marriage. I was about to agree with him, when the Holy Spirit ever so soft and gentle whispered in my right ear, "Be careful how you answer." In that split second I knew what I said next must be very important and I answered "Yes, I can forgive you." That was Grace...that was the Holy Spirit allowing me to put Bill before my own pain.

Bill continues: I left that Thursday night asking myself, "What have I done?" Satan had me on this merry-go-round and had me convinced there was no turning back. My heart was cold and black and I knew I was going to hell, but like they say, "life is too short." The next day all I heard in my head was, "go home, go home." I later found out there were many people praying for me. Later that night, I was in my apartment, surrounded by what I can only describe as evilness. It was such an awful dark, draining feeling. I remembered what Connie had told me, so I fell to the floor and cried out to Jesus for forgiveness. I immediately felt a glow all around me and knew it was the Holy Spirit, and felt the evilness around me leave. I laid on the floor and cried for what seemed like hours. When I got up, I just wanted to go home, but how could I? Now understand, this was January 14, just 48 hours from the time I left home. God said, "Text her." I texted her, and that night I returned home a new man! This began our journey and our ministry of salvation, forgiveness and healing.

> **Connie:** *God has given us hope and strength, so we can extend this to other couples. All things are possible through God, Jesus Christ our Lord and Saviour and the Holy Spirit who leads us.*

Now, six years later, their marriage is stronger than ever. They live with love and forgiveness and have helped many other couples through difficult times. Forgiveness is essential to our wholeness—emotionally, relationally, and spiritually. Jesus knows the power of forgiveness and how important it is for answered prayer.

> *Therefore I tell you, whatever you ask in prayer, believe that you have received it, and it will be yours. And whenever you stand praying, forgive, if you have anything against anyone, so that your Father also who is in heaven may forgive you your trespasses."* Mark 11:24-25 NKJV

Of course, our Father has forgiven us, but often we hold on to bitter unforgiveness towards others and this hinders our faith and our experience of wholeness in our own lives. The Holy Spirit is always ready to reveal any unforgiveness we are harboring and to empower us to forgive those who have hurt us. He knows this will bring freedom and healing to our whole being. Jesus wants us free from unforgiveness in all our relationships.

The Holy Spirit is always ready to reveal any unforgiveness we are harboring and to empower us to forgive those who have hurt us. He knows this will bring freedom and healing to our whole being.

Jesus Wants Us Free from Unhealthy Habits

"Please pray for my knees," the young University of Illinois woman said. "I am in so much pain there are times I can barely walk to class." It was Sunday morning and I, along with another woman, were praying for people after the worship service. Because we only have a few minutes, we don't have the advantage to wait too long on the Holy Spirit to guide our prayers, so we often go right for healing the physical pain. However, I knew I could not do that in good conscience. I wouldn't be doing this young woman any favors by simply laying hands on her knees and commanding the pain to go. Why not? Because she was carrying about one hundred pounds of extra weight. This had an obvious effect on her knee pain which would probably not disappear without her losing some weight. Did I just boldly tell her to lose weight? No. That is a touchy subject and I knew I had to proceed cautiously. I also knew that Jesus wants us whole and that includes our being good stewards of His temple, our bodies. However, when someone struggles with extreme weight issues, I am aware that there are possibly other factors involved—past abuse issues, genetic metabolic problems, depression and yes, an unhealthy lifestyle of poor eating habits. Again, we are a whole, integrated being and we must approach healing in that way. Needless to say, I am thankful for the Holy Spirit who gladly gives us insight and direction, and knows how to bring healing to the whole person. He is good at giving gentle but powerful help in breaking old, unhealthy habits and releasing grace to embrace new, healthy habits of eating, sleeping and exercise so we may be made whole. This young woman was open to an honest discussion about her weight and later chose to have helpful surgery that resulted in a 120 pound weight loss and new strength for her knees, too.

> He is good at giving gentle but powerful help in breaking old, unhealthy habits and releasing grace to embrace new, healthy habits of eating, sleeping and exercise so we may be made whole.

While the Bible writers don't say a great deal about healthy eating and drinking, there are a few cautions:

Be not among drunkards or among gluttonous eaters of meat, for the drunkard and the glutton will come to poverty, and slumber will clothe them with rags. Proverbs 23:20-21 NKJV

All throughout the Old Testament God gave very specific instructions on healthy eating that some even continue today. We are now free to eat as we choose but these restrictions do highlight God's concern for our nutrition. We are wise to watch what we eat, especially in our culture where sugar abounds. There are many good resources today that can help each of us choose the best plan for healthy eating.

And it is very helpful to add a consistent exercise plan to your life. My husband and I have a simple, doable plan of walking just sixty minutes a day in our neighborhood. No transportation, no fee and no extra equipment required (except long johns in the Illinois sub-zero weather!). Our bodies are the very home of God and He is eager for us to cooperate with Him in keeping them strong and healthy. Jesus wants us free from unhealthy habits so we may be made whole.

Good rest and sleep are likewise critical for our health and God made this clear when He instituted the Sabbath (although there are other reasons for this, and of course, we are not under the Old Covenant now). The point is, Father knows best and we cannot sustain a healthy body, mind or spirit if we are not getting good rest and deep sleep. Develop good sleep habits in order to stay healthy, and if needed, receive prayer to heal what may be disturbing your sleep because God gives us good sleep.

In peace I will lie down and sleep, for you alone, O Lord, will keep me safe. Psalm 4:8 NLT

You can go to bed without fear; you will lie down and sleep soundly. . Proverbs 3:24 NLT

Jesus wants us whole—body, mind and spirit—and we can be confident He will show us how to enjoy a full and vibrant long life.

I will reward them with a long life and give them my salvation." Psalm 91:16 NLT

My child listen to me and do as I say, and you will have a long, good life. Proverbs 4:10 NLT

Thank you, Jesus, for making us whole. Thank you for a long and healthy life!

Discussion Questions

1. God's healing is multidimensional: physical, emotional, mental, relational, spiritual and more. Share one way God has brought His healing into your life to move you towards wholeness.

2. Why is it important for us to be healthy and whole in every way? How does this affect our role as Jesus' body here on earth now?

3. What dimension of God's healing are you most in need of in your life today?

Chapter 6

Jesus Sends Us to Heal

The Need for Healing Ministry

Once we begin to make contact with the healing power of Jesus and experience the reality that Jesus Heals Today, our eyes will likely begin to open to the rampant need that exists in our society right now. As our culture slides away from biblical moorings, the need for Jesus' healing power is exponentially growing.

The rate of families fracturing has climbed frighteningly high. It is the exception to be raised to young adulthood without experiencing major family trauma, rather than the general rule. We have, at this point, multiple generations where deep emotional wounding has become the norm, not the exception. Our sexual ethics have run opposite of God's design for close to fifty years, unimpeded, and we are increasingly reaping the fruit of our choices, both culturally, and at times, within our own bodies.

Social media and the internet have not only universalized access to pornographic and other damaging materials, but they have also created an environment where the way we relate to other human beings on a regular basis is less than decent and respectful. Our television shows, movies and video games are rife with violence, hate, sexuality and more. On top of this, the rates of many physical ailments appear to be climbing. Autism seems to be on the rise. Food allergies, while once an abnormality, are far more prevalent. Diabetes and cancer continue to scourge our lives, and obesity has become an epidemic.

Psychological conditions continue to grow as well. Anxiety issues run rampant. Depression and out-of-control anger are increasingly common. Hopelessness and a general apathetic despair is almost accepted as the human condition.

It is easy to look at these as statistics, but these conditions aren't just numbers; we are talking about human lives. We are talking about brokenness, pain and sorrow on massive scales. It's one thing to accept the reality of our broken world if there is no possible solution, but once we begin to see Jesus' healing power as available, the need can be overwhelming.

> Each and every one of us is born with our humanity intertwined with brokenness, and as long as that is the case, our world will have no shortage of opportunities for God's kingdom to break in.

This avalanche of need is not new. It has been around since the exodus from the Garden of Eden. Each and every one of us is born with our humanity intertwined with brokenness, and as long as that is the case, our world will have no shortage of opportunities for God's kingdom to break in.

Jesus Sends the Disciples

Jesus was familiar with this feeling. In the closing verses of Matthew 9, we see Jesus in touch with the reality of the human condition:

And Jesus went throughout all the cities and villages, teaching in their synagogues and proclaiming the gospel of the kingdom and healing every disease and every affliction. When he saw the crowds, he had compassion for them, because they were harassed and helpless, like sheep without a shepherd. Matthew 9:35-36 ESV

Jesus brought healing to every disease and every affliction. There is no condition too hard for Jesus; He is Lord over every one. Seeing the level of need, He saw that people had been harassed by the devil and were helpless. There was no solution available; they wandered like sheep with no guidance or protection. In the midst of seeing immense need, Jesus instructs His followers:

The he said to his disciples, "The harvest is plentiful, but the laborers are few; therefore pray earnestly to the Lord of the harvest to send out laborers into his harvest." Matthew 9:37-38 ESV

This is fascinating to me. Jesus is essentially saying He, alone, is not enough! He has the ability to bring healing, but the need is too overwhelming; there are too many people that need what He has to offer. As a result, Jesus asks for help praying that effective workers would be released to help with the burden.

Jesus came to bring healing to the world. As God incarnate, He is Jehovah-Rapha, the Lord our Healer. He embodies that, along with every other aspect, of God's nature. As powerful as Jesus' healing power is, He was still a finite human vessel. He only had 24 hours in a day and needed to eat and sleep like the rest of us. He hit His human limitations and needed to continue to multiply his impact through another channel.

In the next few verses, we see Jesus change strategies. He would continue to minister in healing, but He also began to release His disciples to bring the same healing:

And he called to him his twelve disciples and gave them authority over unclean spirits, to cast them out, and to heal every disease and every affliction. These twelve Jesus sent out, instructing them, "Go nowhere among the Gentiles and enter no town of the Samaritans, but go rather to the lost sheep of the house of Israel. And proclaim as you go, saying, 'The kingdom of heaven is at hand. Heal the sick, raise the dead, cleanse lepers, cast out demons...'" Matthew 10:1, 5-8 ESV

He sends out His twelve apostles to increase his strategic impact. Now instead of just one person traveling throughout Israel healing the sick, there were thirteen. Luke records the result:

> And they departed and went through the villages, preaching the gospel and healing everywhere. Luke 9:6 ESV

Once the twelve return successfully, having completed their assignment, Jesus mobilizes even more:

> After this the Lord appointed seventy-two others and sent them on ahead of him, two by two, into every town and place where he himself was about to go. Luke 10:1 ESV

There are now eighty-five people bringing the healing and power of the kingdom of God to the Judean countryside. Jesus has multiplied His impact to reach more and more people.

Jesus Healed for Healing's Sake

When I first came across the recorded accounts of healing in the gospels, I assumed what I think many of us assume—that Jesus healed people to prove He was the Messiah. The signs and wonders were meant to be proof that He had come from God and that everyone should listen to Him.

Now I am convinced there is more to the story than that. I do believe Jesus' healing did accomplish that task; it was doubtless proof that He was the Messiah, but the biblical texts show something deeper going on. Jesus healed because He wanted to. He healed because He believed in healing and felt it was important.

Jesus raised up eighty-four others and drafted them to heal the sick. He could have just sent them out to preach or testify of what they had seen, but He didn't. He sent them out because He couldn't personally heal enough people and the need had gripped His heart. We see the same motivation when the twelve return:

> The apostles returned to Jesus and told him all that they had done and taught. And he said to them, "Come away by yourselves to a desolate place and rest a while." For many were coming and going and that had no leisure even to eat. And they went away in the boat to a desolate place by themselves. Now many saw them

going and recognized them, and they ran there on foot from all the towns and got there ahead of them. When he went ashore he saw a great crowd, and had compassion on them, because they were like sheep without a shepherd. And he began to teach them many things. Mark 6:30-34 ESV

Jesus is trying to bring the disciples on a sabbatical. Things have gotten so intense they don't even have time to eat! While trying to get away, the people recognize Jesus and the crew, and a huge crowd gathers ahead of time. When Jesus gets there, the compassion in Him rises up again and even though they're all exhausted, He ministers to the crowd.

Jesus' healings did offer proof He was the Messiah, there is no doubt of that. But there is also no doubt that Jesus didn't heal people just for that proof; He healed people because His heart was moved by their brokenness and He wanted to bring them healing.

A Healing Cause

Jesus had bigger plans yet. His end-game was to launch a worldwide movement that could bring healing to multitudes. He didn't want to just reach those in Israel or even stop with mobilizing eighty-five in the healing ministry; He wanted to bring healing to everyone.

After Jesus brought His healing power to Israel, He began to set His sights higher. He didn't want to stop there. No, in Jesus all the families of the world were to be blessed (Genesis 12:3). So Jesus began to aim for a new target—to bring healing power to world.

As we saw in Chapter 2, Satan was the "ruler of this world" before Jesus came along. Because of Israel's covenant relationship with God, Jesus was able to minister healing and freedom to them without violating the authority structure God had created (and Satan hijacked). But to release that healing power to the rest of the world, Satan would have to be disposed. If Satan could be disposed, Jesus could release healing through the movement of His followers and wrap the globe in the demonstrated power of the kingdom.

So Jesus begins to march toward Calvary, the ultimate showdown with Satan. Along the way, He proclaims the end of the enemy's reign and His intention to impact the entire world.

Now is the judgment of this world; now will the ruler of this world be cast out. And I, when I am lifted up from the earth, will draw all people to myself. John 12:31-32 ESV

Once Satan has been overthrown, Jesus instructs His disciples to no longer limit their terrain to just Israel, but to all nations, and He specifically tells them to pass along the full set of instructions of how to be a disciple (including to heal the sick, raise the dead and so forth).

*And Jesus came and said to them, "All authority in heaven and on earth has been given to me. Go therefore and make disciples of all nations, baptizing them in the name of the Father and of the Son and of the Holy Spirit, **teaching them to observe all that I have commanded you.** And behold, I am with you always, to the end of the age. Matthew 28:18-20 ESV, emphasis mine*

Jesus was raising up a healing people, a worldwide force with the ability to meet the worldwide need.

Jesus clearly intended the pattern of kingdom proclamation and demonstration to continue through every disciple made throughout all the nations. Jesus was raising up a healing people, a worldwide force with the ability to meet the worldwide need.

Our Heritage

You and I are offshoots of this heritage. We flow from the discipleship efforts of the twelve apostles, centuries ago. Generation by generation the kingdom cause has been passed along until today, when it is carried by you and me. We are now the people who have the responsibility to continue to observe all that Jesus commanded the disciples. It is for us today.

Many of us don't feel qualified to carry this call. I know when I first encountered healing, I didn't believe I could be a conduit of Jesus' healing power. I felt that it required a specific gifting or a certain calling to be able to walk in the supernatural. Since I had never experienced supernatural activity, I assumed it wasn't for me. Sure, Jesus wanted to heal the sick, but use me? I doubt it.

There is a paradigm in the church that reinforces this picture; the supernatural ministry of Jesus is for a select few. The gifted, called, anointed or whatever you want to call them. The problem with this paradigm is that it directly absolves us of the responsibility to do what Jesus said.

> Truly, truly, I say to you, whoever believes in me will also do the works that I do; and greater works than these will he do, because I am going to the Father. John 14:12 ESV

Jesus clearly intended the pattern of kingdom proclamation and demonstration to continue through every disciple made throughout all the nations. Jesus was raising up a healing people, a worldwide force with the ability to meet the worldwide need.

Sure, what Jesus is asking you to do seems impossible—of course it is! Jesus doesn't send us to do what we could do without Him, but what only God can do. That is how God is displayed through His body on the earth today.

Do you qualify as someone who believes in Jesus? If so, you have not only the capacity to heal the sick, but the responsibility to be obedient to what Jesus calls us to.

A Simple Tool

Sometimes we can make this whole thing too complicated. When I have the opportunity to pray for someone outside of an environment where it is expected behavior, a whole flood of mind games can set in: *What if they think I'm crazy? What if I pray and nothing happens? How could I possibly pray for them without it being horribly awkward? What do I do?!?!*

The fact remains that there is no risk-free way to partner with the Holy Spirit. In moments when I have the opportunity to minister, I keep trying to find one, but it doesn't seem to work like that. Creating a space and inviting God to show up necessitates that I position myself in a place where I can look really out of touch.

The trajectory I find God taking me on is not one of having sure-fire opportunities. Rather, the Holy Spirit is teaching me to be comfortable in the risk. The Spirit is called the Helper (John 14:26), but learning to position myself in a place where I need His help has been a journey for me.

In reality, most of the time the potential benefit far outweighs the risk. The worst that could happen is that I look silly or a little dumb - something that is bound to happen from time to time anyway! It hasn't killed me yet, and I doubt it ever will. The best that can happen though, is that something absolutely incredible occurs. Jesus could show up and change someone's life forever. The ripple effect of that could affect many lives. It's a bet we would do well to take!

One of the more challenging barriers we have to learn to overcome is stepping out to offer prayer to someone. To most people (even many believers), this will be outside the social norms. This is what can make it so awkward and what sparks fear in us. One of the best things I've found in situations like that is a little advance preparation can go a long way. If I don't feel I'm winging it, I can navigate the uncertain social territory much more easily.

To that end, I'd like to introduce you to a simple little tool Di shared with our church years ago. It's an easy phrase you can lean on to help you cross the bridge and risk seeing Jesus show up. Memorize these seven simple words:

"Can I pray for you right now?"

That's it. That's all you need to ask when the opportunity arises. When someone is complaining of a migraine or sharing about the grief of losing a relationship, you can simply ask, "Can I pray for you right now?" That will get you off the bench and into the game.

One note: those last two words are incredibly important. When people think about prayer, particularly the non-religious types, they often imagine someone kneeling by the side of the bed, hands folded, talking with Jesus. Clarifying that we're talking about something in the moment is really helpful.

I find many times that people are very receptive; what harm could prayer do? Other times people can be confused. They don't really understand what you're offering. If that's the case, I simply explain what it will look like. "Oh, it's not going to be awkward or anything. I'm just going to talk with Jesus and ask for His healing to come to you. No one will even recognize anything is happening other than us talking." Sometimes people will turn me down. If so, that's okay - I've been faithful to my responsibility. Their choices are up to them.

If they say yes, I simply pray a quick prayer, commanding the situation to change, as we see Jesus often prayed. If it seems appropriate, I'll even ask them if they've experienced any change in the condition. Sometimes even with a simple prayer, wild things can happen!

This simple tool has empowered countless prayer encounters all across our community. Tuck it in your back pocket and keep your eyes open for the next opportunity you have to step in and create some room for Jesus to demonstrate His healing power.

Prayer in Action

There is one woman in our church I just can't help but celebrate. Burnsey Eisenmenger has been in our church for many years. She is a retired teacher and is passionate about seeing Jesus heal people.

Burnsey is soft spoken and quiet by nature. She is not the typical person you may envision praying for people in out-of-the-box contexts. Honestly, you'd likely envision her as a librarian before a healing minister.

A number of years ago, Burnsey began to experiment praying for people in public as she saw relevant need. She offered to pray for people she bumped into at the grocery store or around the neighborhood. Before I knew it, Burnsey was ministering to people every single week, just about wherever she went. She was hooked!

After a few years of ministering as she saw opportunity, Burnsey began to dream about demonstrating Jesus' healing on a bigger scale. One thing led to another and she, along with a team of volunteers, was invited to another church in town. Burnsey shared a brief message about healing and each team member shared a testimony. Then they prayed for the sick. Incredible miracles rippled through their meeting.

This invitation led to more invitations. In no time at all, Burnsey was holding regular healing meetings at churches and ministries all over the community. Pastors bring her in to stir up the things of the Spirit in their congregations. Burnsey has now been running these meetings for a number of years. She has impacted countless people through her championing the healing ministry of Jesus, both in the church and out in the community.

My favorite part of this whole story? Burnsey is not on any church staff. She doesn't have a pastoral title or a dramatic stage presence. Instead, she is a normal, everyday gal who is deeply in love with Jesus and boldly pursues releasing His healing power every chance she gets. Because of that, God uses her in ways many pastors only dream of.

Turning the Tide

What would it look like if every believer began to take responsibility to bring the healing power of Jesus to their spheres of influence? We have all be planted in families, neighborhoods and workplaces. What would happen if each and every one of us took responsibility to begin to learn how to effectively heal the sick? What would happen if we took the opportunities that sit right in front of us already? Of course we would not do it perfectly, but all together we have the potential to bring enormous impact to our broken society.

In times of great darkness it is easy to forget the Lord is still at work. Elijah despaired that he was the only prophet left in the land that was true to the Lord. He mourned that all Israel had turned to the false god, Baal (1 Kings 19:14). God responded by informing him there were more than seven thousand in Israel that had remained faithful. Sometimes we can feel the same way; we are the only believer left in our community or workplace.

While it's possible that's true, it is far from likely. The fact is there is still a significant percentage of believers in our land. A lot more than most of us realize. The issue is not that we don't have the people we need to bring the cultural influence we desire, it is that the people we have are ineffectual. We have been silenced; told that it isn't politically correct to share our beliefs or convinced that to expose ourselves as Christians will get us typecast or put up for ridicule.

As a result, thousands upon thousands of believers never make a kingdom difference in their world every week. They get up, live their lives and hit the bed in the evening never having shined their light into the environment around them. The primary issue is actually not that we need more people, we need the people we have to begin to work!

God has given us a great tool, a supernatural tool that has the ability to turn people's lives upside down and demonstrate how good and powerful He really is. Will you take up the call to continue the mission Jesus established? He sends you to heal the sick.

Discussion Questions

1. What is your reaction to the thought that Jesus not only heals today, but that He wants to heal others **through you?**

2. Have you ever experienced Jesus using you to bring healing to someone else? Share the story.

3. What is one step you could take this week to begin to take the next step on the journey of releasing Jesus' healing to others around you?

Conclusion

A Lifelong Journey

An Awakening Church

Not even as many as thirty years ago, much of the church was quite closed to the idea of supernatural ministry. Cessationism, the belief that the gifts of the Holy Spirit are confined to the past, was very prevalent in the church. The suggestion that believers could effectively pray for the sick, drive out demons or prophesy was the kind of thing you only talked about if you wanted to be controversial.

The church as a whole has been shifting in that regard. Whereas in the past the ministry of the Holy Spirit was taboo, now it has become acceptable. Many major evangelical leaders embrace the gifts of the Spirit vocally.

I find this trend encouraging; the church is waking up. We are realizing that Jesus meant for us to be empowered by the Holy Spirit and only then can we be effective as His witnesses:

> *But you will receive power when the Holy Spirit has come upon you, and you will be my witnesses in Jerusalem and in all Judea and Samaria, and to the end of the earth."* Acts 1:8 ESV

In my opinion though, the process is far from completed. While it has become acceptable to believe in healing, belief may still be a far cry from participating in the healing ministry. There ultimately isn't much difference in believing in healing or not if you do nothing with it.

> While it has become acceptable to believe in healing, belief may still be a far cry from participating in the healing ministry.

Scripture is unambiguous that faith is always carried out in actions. If the actions are missing, we are misled to say we have faith:

> *You see that faith was active along with [Abraham's] works, and faith was completed by his works...For as the body apart from the spirit is dead, so also faith apart from works is dead.* James 2:22, 26 ESV

Jesus envisioned a movement of followers that walk in the power of the Holy Spirit and bring His healing to the world around them. You and I are invited into that movement.

Following Jesus means making a lifestyle of learning to heal. He is the ultimate healer and becoming His disciple means taking a lifelong journey of learning how to cooperate with what the Holy Spirit is doing to release Jesus' healing. This book may be the first step in your journey, or just one more step in a road that stretches through years of your life. Either way, the road is there for the taking, beckoning to all who follow the Lord. Will you choose to be obedient to His call?

Some Potential Next Steps

God will guide us along this path. He will direct us to mentors, books, classes or conferences that may help us, if we will ask for His direction. Remember, God never asks something of us that He has not planned to empower us to do. As we step out in obedience, we are met by His grace and guidance.

One of the most effective steps for many people is to find a mentor who can equip and train you in the healing ministry. As we said before, John Wimber, the founder of the Vineyard movement, used to say that supernatural ministry is "more caught than taught"–meaning that effective practice needs to come through being in the environment where we can see it in action. I know in my life that's been critical.

Books can also be incredibly helpful tools in this journey. We hope this book has been just that for you! Some other books you might consider are:

- **Power Healing** – John Wimber
  A classic book written by the Vineyard founder John Wimber. Covers many different aspects of healing.

- **Doing Healing** – Alexander Venter
  A very thorough and complete book about healing written by a Vineyard pastor after many years of working in the healing ministry.

- **School of Kingdom Ministry Student Manual** – Putty Putman
  A book that discusses the Spirit-empowered life and the role of healing ministry within it.

- **The Essential Guide to Healing** – Randy Clark & Bill Johnson
  An entry-level book on healing by two of the greats. Excellent chapters about testimony, words of knowledge, and a five-step prayer model.

- **Hello Holy Spirit** – Dianne Leman
  An introduction to the Holy Spirit and how He empowers us to live the Christian life.

If it makes sense for your church to participate in School of Kingdom Ministry, we have found that to be an incredibly effective tool for training and releasing people in the healing ministry. School of Kingdom Ministry partners with churches that host their own classes to equip people in their community. Thousands around the globe have participated and seen great fruit. If you are a pastor looking to see this ministry increase in your church, we don't know of a better tool out there. For more information on the School of Kingdom Ministry and how it works, visit **http://schoolofkingdomministry.org**.

The annual More Love More Power conference is also a wonderful place to be in a Spirit-saturated environment and see healing happen. God often makes wonderful deposits in people through conferences like this. You'll be inspired, refreshed and equipped to go to the next level. To learn more, visit **http://morelovemorepower.org**.

The Road Ahead

J.R.R. Tolkien captures the uncertainty of a new adventure infamously as he pens the words of wisdom from Bilbo Baggins to his nephew Frodo:

> *"It's a dangerous business, Frodo, going out your door. You step onto the road, and if you don't keep your feet, there's no knowing where you might be swept off to."*

The road ahead always seems dangerous, and indeed, to walk the path of the healing ministry of Jesus one will face pain, fear and uncertainty. It requires putting ourselves in a place of risk and giving God room to show up in incredible ways. It will also be filled with rejoicing, gratitude and the thrill of adventure. All along the way, we can trust the ride, because we know we are in the hands of a good Father who directs our steps as we submit to Him. We can trust that He will keep our feet underneath us.

In closing, I would like to pray this blessing over you:

> *Father, I thank you for this son/daughter. I thank you that you love them so fully and richly that Jesus found it a joy to trade the sufferings of the cross for the fullness of their redemption. Holy Spirit, I thank you that now you look to empower them to continue to extend the kingship of Jesus and use them to destroy the works of the devil.*

> *I bless your eyes to be open to see what the Lord is doing. I bless your ears to hear His voice. I bless your heart to rest secure in His love and your steps to always be in step with His. May you be sensitive to the Spirit of God and may you have the courage to step out in risk and partner with Him. I bless you to see the healing ministry of Jesus made real in your life, as He lives in you now. May many come to His wholeness through your journey.*

Appendix

Sample Prayers

This appendix provides some sample prayers to help get you started in praying for healing for others. Always remember, the power isn't in the method; it's in the person you are praying to. While these prayers follow the biblical pattern, we always need to be open to the Holy Spirit's guidance and direction in any specific prayer encounter.

Praying for Physical Healing

The biblical pattern for praying for physical healing is to speak to the condition and command it to change. This is probably the simplest type of condition to pray for.

As you begin any healing prayer, invite the presence of the Holy Spirit and allow some time for His presence to manifest. Then, unless you feel otherwise led, command the condition to change in the appropriate way as specifically as possible.

Prayer for arthritic knees:

Come, Holy Spirit. We welcome your presence...(wait)

I release healing to these knees right now. I command arthritis to leave and take all the pain with you. I release the knees from aching, swelling and I bless them to move fully with no pain.

After praying, it's often helpful to check in and see if the condition has changed at all. Remember, there is no rule that you can only pray once. If any measure has changed, keep praying until things stop changing with prayer..

Praying for Emotional Healing

Emotional healing often involves releasing emotional pain the person is carrying, or inviting Jesus to come and bring truth to where the person has believed their history instead of Jesus. It can feel more like an art than a science, but the rule of thumb is to identify where a person's emotional life is not in alignment with Jesus and bring them to the Lord to ask for His healing. Sometimes this means you pray specific prayers over them and sometimes it means you guide the person in releasing their past, their hurt and their emotional burdens to the Lord:

Prayer for releasing the pain of abuse as a child:

Come, Holy Spirit. We welcome your presence...(wait)

God, I release peace over Tom right now. I bless him to be able to dwell in your love and your goodness. God, I ask that right now all the pain from being abused by his father growing up would begin to come up and out, that he can live in your love.

I ask that you would open his heart up, God. Open his heart to your goodness. Open his heart to your kindness and your compassion over his life.

[Directing Tom] Would you like to release the pain to God? Pray this with me:
"God, I give this pain to you. I release the pain of the abuse I experienced and I put those painful feelings in your hands. I choose

to live in peace and I choose to trust you. Thank you that you are good and I don't have to protect myself from you."

[Resuming prayer] Father, I thank you that your goodness. Every bit of that pain from the past, right now I command it to let him go and to leave. I bless you with the freedom Jesus has for you.

As you pray for emotional healing, you want to keep your eyes open and be aware if emotions are releasing (you probably won't miss them). As the Holy Spirit ministers, it's common for the person to experience deep emotions while God rearranges things.

Praying to Forgive Others

Many of us carry around some unforgiveness towards others. While it may initially make us feel powerful, the fact is that in the long run it is only destructive to us. Lack of forgiveness is often connected to the need for physical or emotional healing, and deliverance as well.

When guiding a person to forgive someone, you have to take that person through the prayer; you can't forgive someone on their behalf–they have to make the choice. You can make it easier by giving them the words, though. Once you have taken them through the process, you'll want to pray to release any effect the unforgiveness may have had on them.

Prayer for forgiving a friend of gossip:

Come, Holy Spirit. We welcome your presence...(wait)

[Directing Sue] Repeat after to me with this prayer:
"God, I choose to forgive Jack for gossiping about me to the family. That hurt me deeply, but I choose to let him go and I release that to you. God, I ask that you would take that sin he did against me and you would deal with it."

[Resuming prayer] Jesus, I thank you that your forgiveness extends to all who ask. We release and bless Jack and we ask for your will to fully come to pass in his life. Right now I release Sue from every effect that unforgiveness has had in her life, body, mind and spirit. I bless her with wholeness and your life.

Praying to Repent for Sin

Praying people through repentance for sin is important in two cases: first, when they are deciding to change paths and discontinue to participate in sin, and second, when they are struggling to experience their forgiveness. Often we may know that Jesus has forgiven us, but we still feel guilty. In this instance, you're helping someone experience forgiveness. There are parts of us that learn by experience and experiencing the forgiveness Jesus has extended to us can be very restorative.

This, again, is the kind of prayer you have to guide the person through praying for themselves. Have a conversation about the issue and make sure they are ready to choose to repent of their own will, then guide them through the process:

Prayer for repentance from bitterness

Come, Holy Spirit. We welcome your presence...(wait)

[Directing Phil] Pray this along with me:
"*God, I see now that I have been bitter toward my mother. The way she treated me when I grew up was painful to me and it felt humiliating. I have chosen to be bitter, but right now I choose a different road. I'm sorry for holding bitterness in my life. I let go of my mother and her choices and I choose to be content with the life you have given me, trusting you can give me everything I need, even if my mother didn't do that growing up. Jesus, thank you that you offer to me forgiveness when I give you my sin. I give bitterness to you, and I receive your forgiveness.*"

[Resuming prayer] *I bless you to receive the forgiveness of the Lord. God washes you clean and pure and removes the sin of bitterness as far as the east is from the west. Let the cleansing of the Holy Spirit come and release every bit of the poison that has dwelled within your heart.*

Praying for Deliverance

Both prayer for emotional issues and deliverance can be vast and complicated topics. Demons often gain access to people by the person choosing to cooperate with some form of sin. Common examples could be anger, fear, hopelessness, sexual immorality and even idol worship (this list is far from exhaustive). Not every sin winds up with someone demonized—it often happens through a pattern or sin, or a specific commitment to it, so I don't usually assume people are demonized unless they are experiencing something abnormal.

The key for deliverance is to break the agreement with whatever caused the need for deliverance in the first place. This often looks like repentance from sin, possibly forgiveness of others, and verbally choosing a different road. Once that has happened, command the demon to leave:

Prayer for deliverance from a spirit of anger

Come, Holy Spirit. We welcome your presence...(wait)

[Directing Jane] Would you pray this with me?
"God, I'm sorry for agreeing with anger. I have chosen to use anger to dominate other people and be powerful, but I know that is not your way. I turn from that path and I embrace the path of peace. God, I ask you to grow your peace in my life as I submit to you."

[Resuming prayer] Thank you, Jesus, as your peace and your forgiveness wash over Jane right now. I command the spirit of anger to leave. Come out of Jane and go. You are not welcome here; she belongs to Jesus.

As you pray to cast the demon out, stay in tune with the person. As demons leave, there is almost always a way to know they've left. Sometimes the person just feels a darkness lift off of them. Other times they my shudder, burp, cough or more. Either way, when demons leave, you usually know it, and until they leave, you usually can sense the battle. Stick with it and continue to follow the Lord's direction until the person has found freedom.

Acknowledgments

Jesus Heals Today

We live in a messy, sick and hurting world. Because there is so much pain and suffering, it is good news to know that Jesus heals today. It is even better to experience Jesus' healing love and power together with others. Healing happens best in a family—a church community of fellow believers who pray, encourage, instruct and help one another to live the healthiest lives possible. Likewise, this book only happened because a team of believers joined together to communicate our passion that Jesus Heals Today. First, our preaching team prayed, studied and proclaimed this truth in six weekend messages. Thanks to Clay Harrington, Julie Yoder and Happy Leman who joined Putty and myself in delivering those messages that became the core content of the six chapters of the book.

We are thankful, too, for our video production and communication team of Laura Bice, Derek Manson, Ashton Harwood, Dusten Jenkins, Jess Smuk and Katie Goulet who collaboratively produced great graphics, and a super DVD of teaching and testimonies to accompany Jesus Heals Today. We are both so grateful for all the men, women and children who joined in our church-wide study of Jesus Heals Today and shared their stories of experiencing Jesus' healing. We saw many wonderful healings and learned much together, even when healing did not happen.

Shelly Manning was a fantastic editor and Jody Boles did a great job of formatting all our work. Since we cannot even begin to do what they did, we say a big thanks to them for making this book readable and attractive, too.

Both Putty and I have amazing spouses who support our writing habit. Thanks to Brittany and Happy for encouraging us, understanding our moods and loving us through all the ups and downs. They are such a valuable part of this book and we could not have done it without them.

And of course...Thank you, Holy Spirit, for opening our eyes and hearts to experience Jesus as Healer. He has changed our lives, healed our bodies and loved us with His unfailing love. Our prayer is for all our readers to know– Jesus Heals Today.

89465518R00065

Made in the USA
Columbia, SC
15 February 2018